WAR PILOT MEMOIRS: A MIRROR ON 1939

by
Jacques Drabier

Translated by
J. Anomdeplume

Copyright © 2010 Adelif Inc., an Arizona Corporation
All rights reserved under International and
Pan-American Copyright Conventions.

Published in the United States by
Serey/Jones Publishers, Inc.
www.sereyjones.com

ISBN: 978-1-881276-13-5

the authors:
    Drabier, Jacques
    Anomdeplume, J.
    Jacques, P.
    Hodges, John D.

Table of Contents

Translator's Comments v

Chapter 1
Grand Destiny with Viet Beginnings 1

Chapter 2
My Youth: Pre-War Paris, 1930s 19
Patriarchal Decision: France

Chapter 3
War Breaks: 1940, I am Seventeen 39

Chapter 4
Quote: "Do We just Yield, into Custom-made Nooses?" 59
Our Escape aboard a Lobster Boat

Chapter 5
Deployed to Arabia 77

Chapter 6
Anti-sabotage by Camelback, Improvised Bombs . 85

Chapter 7
Bristol-Blenheims, those old *Potez* and American Monocoupes 97

Chapter 8
My Head in a Basket <u>or</u>
Narrow Escape . . . like James Bond 103

Chapter 9
Swimming Pool Romance 113

Chapter 10
The Flying Snake 121

Chapter 11
A Live Bomb for a Hockey Puck 125

Chapter 12
Air Crafts: Not Identifiable 137

Chapter 13
Chivalry in the Skies 143

Chapter 14
Post-War Wedding Bells: Wine, not Beer 151

Chapter 15
Small Game Hunts in German Forests &
Reports of Japanese Acts 159

Chapter 16
Back in France, & Surprise: Maritime Saigon 165

Chapter 17
A Precious Soul enters our World 173
1946 Sees Me back in Indochina

Chapter 18
Curare, Cobras, and Tiger Cubs 179

Chapter 19
The Las Vegas of the Orient 189

Chapter 20
A Precious Soul enters Heaven 205

Chapter 21
Dénouement: Nightmares on
a Danish Cargo Ship 219

Acknowledgements 223

UN INCROYABLE DESTIN
Volume I
« Miroir d'un passé glorieux »

War Pilot Memoirs:
A Mirror on 1939

Translator's Comments:
A Mission to Pass Jacques' Experience on to Future Generations

It was over a glass of Armagnac, a liqueur, that Jacques succinctly expressed to me the spirit of this book as a *prise d'un journal légèrement romancée*, as a rendition of a diary lightly seasoned to become a novel.

That was after my complimenting whatever little angel had sat upon his shoulder to inspire this perfect mix of 1930s historical perspectives and first-person accounts of in-flight combat and tiger hunts a decade later.

Would the true historian in each of us rather read about a young Frenchman in a 1938 archery contest against our "Fritz", or about statistics? Wouldn't the romantic in each of us prefer bedtime reading about a real life cloak-and-dagger in Damascus versus any other? Don't many of us want to learn the thoughts of a fighter pilot, ammunition depleted, as he ducked under the wing of a Flying Fortress?

*   *   *

As if listening to all the best war stories your grandfather or another veteran might have told you, turn these pages, dear Reader, with enthusiasm. It is a global odyssey, with an intriguing uneven flow as if notes scribbled into a journal, and it is cliffhanger non-fiction.

J. Anomdeplume
JohnHodges@global.t-bird.edu
Phoenix, Arizona 2009

This book is dedicated to
Janine Borski-Drabier, my Guardian Angel.
She is a neurosurgical research clinician by profession.
Thanks to her myriad abilities in health care,
she helps me to survive.
Because she possesses excellent writing skills,
she assisted me in writing my memoirs.
Her devotion and her faith as a loving partner
have created happiness in our marriage.
The Divine Power has protected us and
blessed the union of our hearts.

– Jacques Drabier

War Pilot Memoirs: A Mirror on 1939

CHAPTER 1

Grand Destiny with Viet Beginnings

When we speak of destiny, of fate, what do we mean? Definitions should include this concept: circumstances which influence events. These are simply deviations in the course of things which result in a beneficial or detrimental outcome. Sometimes such a deviation can be part of a set of circumstances over which we exercise no control, and what follow are consequences: oft positive, oft negative.

It is generally believed that the human course of events is predestined, that we are following a path already laid out for us. This theory, acceptable though it may be, needs to account for how destiny gets influenced by points of karma. In the evolution of mankind, "karma" simply acknowledges the relationships between causes and effects. We proclaim events which must have occurred in some prior life cycle as renewing themselves now.

An important part of this Destiny, then, is karma, and we see therein the same coordinates, the same spiritual rendezvous locations, seen in the past. Don't be fooled! We possess the power to modify this karma, to steer it, or to correct these "points" of karma when we become aware of them. It is thusly that we improve our lives. At times, Destiny will pursue her whims, her capricious turns, and all we can do is hang on for dear life! With these statements as a basis, I now proceed to tell you how Destiny has never ceased bringing me to the proverbial lip of the precipice, to the cutting edge of many an adventure.

Preamble

It is with complete sincerity that I compose my memoirs, constantly forcing myself to remember details just as clearly as I can. I call upon documentary evidence whenever possible, but unfortunately this is not always available, the better part of my records having been lost to the Indochinese War of the early 1950s. When the French were expelled, the majority of my possessions got destroyed. As I write to the best of my recollection, I try to present facts and events in the simplest possible way, all in conserving their true nature and importance. For example, I was denied access, at gunpoint, to land that I owned in Indochina, and it was important to understand their perceiving <u>me</u> as the enemy.

I describe my adventures as if reliving them, with plenty of passion and emotion. The long and winding road of my life has taken me into countries with "unusual" cultures, though we really should simply say "different" cultures. The differences were often acute for me, finding myself cornered… trapped with no way out! Usually these adventures had unforeseeable outcomes, as adventure gave way to poignant drama, which overwhelmed even me sometimes. I have faced death several times.

I believe in the Universal Creative Force which created us immortal. It is a credo for me that we, as a unique species, have limitless intelligence which will never cease developing and growing bigger.

Reflecting

Typically I do not dream at night, and thus my life is generally peaceful from sundown to sunup. However, one particular Saturday morning in June, 2002, I awoke with a burden on my mind. Seated at the edge of my bed, I experienced a strange sensation as thoughts whirred like tornadoes in my head. My eyes closed… am I dreaming? I heard a voice saying, "The time has come to write your memoirs." The voice came out of nowhere and of course this perplexed me. I decided to put my head under cold water to wake the heck up!

It was a typical Saturday, a day for doing chores, and through the window I saw my wife in the yard. Suddenly, the voice made itself heard with, "The time has come to write your memoirs. Don't forget. Get started right away."* All of this was a bit much, and the voice was very authoritative. I looked all around and there was nobody there, which made me shiver. It was a man's voice which I did not recognize. I tried putting it out of my mind as I went about my daily tasks, not mentioning this to anyone, not even to my wife. I remained intrigued, though, with this order-giving voice.

Several times, friends had already suggested putting my odyssey of a life to paper. It was always with a polite smile that I reacted, saying, "Who in the world would really be interested in the story of my life?"

I know that I've had an active life, full of undertakings, with many an intrepid voyage: a life, I'll grant you, plenty different from the lives of others. I could not help thinking, though, that there must be thousands of folks who've had adventures and who have a bunch of stories to relate.

All my excuses seemed perfectly valid to me. "Me? Write a book? I've got no literary background." Minuses outweighed the pluses, and as the years passed I managed to forget about it. From time to time, a person here and there tried to put the deal back on the table, but without much success.

Friday, December 5th, 2003, was the day of our annual reunion: P-47 Thunderbolt Fighter Pilots. For the heaviness of that propeller-driven airplane, it was known as the "Jug", a cute misnomer since it was just this step-up in firepower that would win the war. There were about a hundred of us "Jug pilots" in the western U.S. and we were meeting in Palm Springs, California. My trip from Phoenix, short compared to others', was filled with happy

---

* « Il est temps d'écrire tes mémoires. Ne l'oublie pas. Commence au plus vite. »

anticipation as we always have a grand old time seeing each other again. There is generally a celebrity who gets invited to speak, and this particular year we had a good surprise in the presence of Brigadier General William Anders, astronaut of Apollo Eight, whose flights had stretched to the Moon and ten times around it. I found him to be a simple, likeable man. He recounted for us, in great detail, the progressive stages that go into lunar flight, a recounting which varied plenty from what the media had told us, with their reports full of both errors and untruths.

The Apollo 8 mission was apparently a troubled one from the get-go. Liftoff was a demarcation of a whole set of bad circumstances, as problem after problem presented itself. Those three guys really had to wonder if they were going to make it back safe and sound.

What an interesting speech, and then he stopped by each of our tables, talking with everybody, giving his valuable time to listen to our exploits which seemed to interest him greatly. "What did **you** do in the war? Which squadron were **you** with? What kind of missions did you fly?" and so forth. He came over to our table and noticed my accent, mistaking it for a German one! It was the epitomizing moment of his evening to learn I was French. With a big grin, he asked my permission to give my wife a kiss on the cheek, adding, "It's not very often I get the chance to embrace a pretty French blonde." My wife was overjoyed to be kissed by an astronaut.

He turned toward me, then, and he looked fascinated to hear what my fighter pilot service had entailed. He looked me straight in the eye, put his hand on my shoulder, and said, "My dear friend, will you please promise me, on your honor, that you're going to write all of this down? Memoirs like yours are crucial to future generations. They need to know how their ancestors fought for the nation, for freedom and for peace. This way, hopefully our children and grandchildren won't repeat the same scenario."

Given that the group gets together once a year, it is pretty noticeable that one or more may turn up missing. We're all pushing ninety years of age or more, and in about ten years no one will be left to explain, in person, the details of that terrible war which swallowed up many thousands of brave souls, people who sacrificed their lives for their countries and for peace among nations.

I made the solemn promise, then, to Brigadier General William Anders to set myself to the task. The request came from such a distinguished man. I was in admiration of this man who had run the gauntlet of a glorious path. He was bringing himself down to my level to tell me, quite simply, the importance which my life represented in the big scheme of things.

*   *   *

Having thought things through, now was the time to heave ho, to gather onto paper the extraordinary stages of the life I've lived. To start, I turned to my ancestors and their origins. I needed to explain what Indochina, known nowadays as Vietnam, was all about.

On my father's side, my great grandfather was from the region of Alsace, that part of modern France which, with Lorraine, has historically been bounced back and forth to Germany. A colonial, he was Governor of the very large State of *Tonkin* [rhymes with Chopin], now in northern Vietnam. Prior to the Great War of 1914 to 1918, there were many people from Alsace who, in order to avoid the risk of being laden with a German yoke, went off as colonials to Indochina and to Algeria.

My paternal grandfather in his turn was Alsace-born too. After World War I, Alsace returned to French control. This grandfather was one of the biggest import-export entrepreneurs of Hanoi, which was in Tonkin. He traveled all the time, and this explains how it is that my father, René Drabier [pronounce drah-BYAI], was born in the town of Blida, Algeria, in northern Africa, formerly a part of France. That was 1887, thirty-five years before my birth. My father did study Law in Algeria yet soon enough found himself back in Indochina. It was in or near the city of Haiphong, in Tonkin, where he met my mother.

On my mother's side, things are a bit obscure as regards her mother's mother. I know my great grandmother was born in the city of Hanoi in the early 1800s. Her parents were both Tonkinese. She married a Frenchman, thus my mother's mother was *métisse*, fifty-fifty Asian and French.

In her own turn, my mother's mother married another Frenchman and they had three girls: Virginie, nicknamed Nini, my mother Pauline, and the youngest one Betty. They also had two boys: Auguste Châtel and André Châtel. These Eurasian siblings, then, had twenty-five percent Asiatic blood in their veins.

My mother, in turn, married my father, a Frenchman, and I am their only child, Jacques Paul Drabier. Thus my blood is one eighth from Indochina, the forerunner of modern Vietnam.

*   *   *

I was born on June 3rd, 1922, in *Cochinchine* [rhyming with Chopin +"SHEEN"], a southern state of Indochina, in a little town called Vinh-long on the Mekong River. Now Vinh-long is in southern Vietnam near Hô Chi Minh City, which was the city of Saigon in my day. My father practiced law there, as a defense attorney at that time.

In good colonial tradition, it was customary to have one's own individual nurse, a nanny, from the time of one's birth. Mine was Chinese, and we called her "Assam." To me she was a second mother. Being constantly in her company, I spoke Chinese. With Mom I spoke Annamite, especially since it was the language of our household staff; this language would nowadays be called Vietnamese. It was less than often that I spoke any French, to the grand disappointment of my father! Hmpf.

Like most colonials we had many household employees: cook, maid, gardener, chauffeur, and all of these had daughters who knew how to sew. My mother set these young women to making things like tablecloths, lace, bedcovers and curtains.

The chauffeur served my father primarily, and this leads me to tell a story to explain why my father never drove. It was not

Chapter 1 *Grand Destiny with Viet Beginnings*

because he was haughty; it was just by necessity. Papa had never taken driving lessons, you see, yet he was of the impression that it was surely the simplest thing in the world.

One day, for the first time ever, he slid into the driver's seat of his car. This luxurious Citroën [pronounce sih-tro-ENN], front wheel drive, was parked in front of the six support columns of the veranda at my Uncle Gott's house. In order to get the car out of there it would be necessary to put it into reverse. My father started the car, stomped on the pedal for the changing of gears causing enough noise to send dogs running off, then pushed on the accelerator just as one should, but perhaps a bit too strongly. Thinking he had engaged the reverse gear as needed, he was actually in a forward gear. Of course he slammed right into one of the six columns. Not only did he tear up the column but he crunched the whole front of the car as it came to an immediate halt. A bunch of us – several friends, my uncle and I – were right there in front of the house. We were stricken with uncontrollable laughter! You should have seen my papa's face, humiliated and vexed, swearing that never ever again would he get behind a steering wheel. He kept this promise, since I never again saw him drive, yet the most amusing aspect of the story is how his proper place was always right there next to the chauffeur, indicating not only which way to go but likewise the proper speed, plus what to do and what not to do. Poor Papa; I miss him. He was a formidable man, righteous and honest and with a certain old school discipline.

My father was much appreciated by his clients, generally the high-society bourgeoisie of Chinese origin. He saved several of them from life imprisonment for certain crimes they had supposedly committed. Later he became Advocate General at the Supreme Court of Saigon. After retiring in France, he set himself up as a caretaker of fine art. The French system of auctioning such pieces requires that an attorney or an ex-attorney be the auctioneer, since art collections often come with disputed ownership.

* * *

So it was in this southern part of Indochina, this *Cochinchine*, where I took my first steps, where I grew up. I really loved this country and the way its countryside appeared, and I admired the indigenous people there, called Annamites. There was a State of Annam which stretched from south to north. Depending on what season it was you could count on a different flavor of perfume in the air which came from exotic flowers and from the national tree, the banyan. In the parks where I went walking you'd see the flamboyant red of this tree, and when these red flowers fell upon the green grass, seeing as how we had plenty of windy days, we kids got rewarded with a plush red rug.

Another stark memory is the sounds you'd hear running around on the verandas: it was like the sound of a hiccup. This particular noise was acute, and it was actually the croaking of little lizards. There were thousands of them, stuck up there on the ceiling of the veranda, sucking in all the mosquitoes they could grab, this being their only food. Picture, if you will, a whole colony of lizards calling back and forth to each other with a hiccupping sound. Among them you could always find a chieftain, the leader of the pack we nicknamed "the Tockey." He was three times as big as a regular size lizard. To make his presence known, he would set off repeating a series of hiccup sounds, once every second or so and very rhythmically, then accelerating. Just like his compadres he nourished himself on mosquitoes, to the great delight of the human inhabitants, since Saigon and the surrounding areas were full of lakes and rivers. I recall sleeping under a large mosquito net, which, in theory, kept insects from devouring us as we slept.

Yet another memory is a culinary and olfactory one: ahhh, that precious aroma of oriental cooking, literally one that followed you everywhere. I can still see myself at age seven, loving that smell and how it would wake up an appetite in me at any hour of the day. My nanny, Assam, would say, "Jacquot [pronounce jah-KOHH], we're going shopping." I had come to know there would always be something good after a shopping trip! We would set out via rickshaw, destined for a trip to fulfill all the little duties that needed doing. This two-wheel vehicle had a seat mounted high that was really very comfortable. Along the sides were two long poles which led forward from the seat and which were joined at the front end by an iron piece turned crossways. A rickshaw driver positioned himself between the wooden members and pulled the rickshaw at a trot. In case of rain there was a folding canopy and a waterproof screen which hung along the sides and the front to protect our legs. These drivers were really devoted and took you anywhere you wanted to go, all for the equivalent of a bowl of rice.

The shopping done, it was time to revel in the pleasure of an "ambulatory" restaurant. "Tic tac... tac, tac" was the advertising racket that came from this merchant walking around offering his very fine soup. Each cook had a musical signature. He'd attract his clientele by tapping with a bamboo rod upon a half-coconut shell. He lugged around heavy equipment, even as he kept his rhythmic drum set going. The equipment consisted of two towers with several shelves constructed of bamboo, and the two towers were balanced across his shoulders on a crossbeam of bamboo which was solid yet flexible. On one side or the other, near the bottom, he had a little stove that burned wood. Upon this stove sat a kettle filled with nicely spiced bouillon which was the base for his soup. One level up in the shelving you would see a wooden plate which served for chopping ingredients: meat, vegetables, you name it. On a lower level in one of the towers there could be found a series of flacons which held all his spices, varying greatly by color and aroma. One particular bottle always contained *nioc-mam*, a superb concoction made by very special procedure, and from a particular species of fish, into a brine sauce. It was used on meat and fish, and it was used to season the soup to the taste of the client.

All up and down the other tower there were drawers containing bowls, thin crusty bread loaves, and seasonings like jasmine, lotus and "jack-fruit" of the *jaquier* tree. Of course these drawers were big enough to carry noodles and rice, plus hot peppers, ginger root and other Chinese delicacies, including those glorious herbs like cilantro. Whenever an interested patron waved down the strolling chef, the chef would delicately poise his equipment on the ground and go to work fixing whichever soup the client preferred. The soup was served up quickly and plenty hot, but, best of all, perfectly seasoned. You could see happy clients with their little bowls, crouched down everywhere alongside the road, in the process of devouring the contents. It was of particular importance to make plenty of noise with one's mouth in order to compliment the cook.

Once satisfied that he had a happy client, the wandering chef would close all the little drawers, fold up shop and carefully organize the load on his shoulders again. Off he went in search of another hungry client, tapping once again on the half-coconut shell with that unique and distinctive rhythm which identified him amongst others. Armed with the same equipment, there were many wandering chefs, each carrying unique ingredients.

Especially in the summertime you'd find merchants purveying cold drinks in the form of shaved ice which they'd pile up in your cup before pouring syrup on top. These sweet liquids came in many colors and the flavors were marvelous and varied. Within this commerce you'd find a wandering knife-and-scissors sharpener. There existed a multitude of wandering merchants since few could afford to have a shop. Poor but proud, they chose to earn their livings honestly. The wandering guys had no taxes to pay yet they were indeed required to have a license. The government sanitation officials inspected the cooks from time to time, since we all knew that proper hygiene was not always top on their list.

From time to time you'd come across an *homme à tout faire*, a universal handyman who would tackle anything. He'd be carrying all his tools on a two-wheel barrow with long handles, and his wrenches and hammers were in a closed compartment. His anvil and grinding wheel were affixed to the cart, and he had a manual hand drill. It functioned by rapidly turning a hand crank which transferred, via thin belts or strings, the turning force to make holes. He was prepared for any assignment from a missing brick in a wall to meticulous trim-carpentry.

The Monsoon Season

Seasonally, by time periods which tended to last about three months, we had strong winds with a bunch of rain, but it was likewise the most atmospherically perfumed time of the year. The smell of each and every flower would get accentuated by abundant rain, and once it started, boy, there descended upon us veritable tons of water. Unfortunately the region was not equipped with any run-off network. With no storm sewers, every street became a river. The water would be at almost two feet deep in fifteen minutes of time, which of course interrupted traffic, but surprisingly not the rickshaw drivers. Those noble souls continued chugging along. Since the seats on the rickshaws were positioned high up, there was not much risk of getting your pants wet in the "river." These guys had legs of steel, and they tugged with jumping steps as they went through the water.

For the kids these flooded streets became playgrounds. Suddenly they would appear out of nowhere, half-naked and laughing, singing or jumping for joy in the way that only little kids can. They played at splashing each other; indeed, this became very much the ritual just as soon as rain started to fall. Needless to say, being a child of prim upbringing, I was forbidden to participate in these bouts of joy. One particular time at about age six, my nanny and I were upon the sidewalk waiting for this torrential rain to subside when I found myself envying the little Indochinese kids having so much fun. Suddenly I broke away and, gleefully crying out in their own tongue, ran to join them, seeking my own share of this childhood bliss. They accepted me into their group with splashing directed at me. I was lightly dressed in shorts, a white shirt and sandals, so quickly enough I was drenched to the bone. Yet, there was glee in my heart.

When the rain stopped, this crowd of kids disappeared. I went walking back to where my nanny was, and boy she was in a furor. While, with one hand, Assam brandished her umbrella at me (above my head, though), I noticed she had to use the other hand to hold up her taffeta pantaloons to keep them dry. All the while she was giving me the sternest chewing-out in Chinese, the language she used on me whenever I'd been bad. Needless to say I was unable to escape the spanking, which soon enough was duplicated by my mother. In my heart I knew I deserved this spanking, but this did not take away the innermost pleasure I had experienced with the Asian kids. This magnificent image of my childhood is precious to me now in my older years, and the image will bring me gratification for the rest of my days.

Nanny in Panic: Child Overboard!

In 1926, in the town of Vinh-long, we were living on a gorgeous estate, and on the back side of the house there was a terrace which looked out upon the river, the Mekong. I was four years old, so my nanny and I still shared a bedroom. For reasons unknown, I had become a sleepwalker. My nanny, who was aware of this, found that it was not important enough to bother my parents with it. I never walked very far, simply sliding out of bed to promenade around the room, hands held out and eyes closed, mumbling. My Assam, who slept lightly, knew just the right method for intervening. Speaking softly, she would gently take hold of my hand. She would hum a song as she guided me back to bed. She would stay there awhile, on the edge of my bed, caressing my hair. I never did resist, and I'd go back to sleep soon enough.

One particular night my nanny must have been sleeping more profoundly than usual, since she had not come to realize that I was missing from my bed. I had managed, without mischievous intent, to get away. The terrace door had not been latched. I guess that Assam awoke by intuition to find my bed empty. To her great shock and dismay she found me balanced atop the little exterior wall on the terrace! How in the world had this little boy been able to scale that wall, taller than he was, and get up there to walk along the top with nothing but the river on the other side?

There I was, walking calmly, balanced, and, yes, my arms were outstretched. She came to realize that I was in a trance and that she certainly didn't want to upset or scare me; I'll bet she almost fainted. Ever so gently she took my hand, speaking very calmly, as she brought me to her bosom. I'm sure that deep inside she was saying, "My dear God, help me," because, had she failed to take my hand, her little Jacki would have fallen off the other side. Having recovered me, she kissed my eyelids and she cried. She put me back into bed and did not dare to leave my side for the balance of the night. From that time onward, the terrace door was certainly locked at nighttime.

Assam finally decided to inform my parents as to my episodes of somnambulism, yet without mentioning the incident on the terrace wall. I was entirely her responsibility, so she felt culpable. Just the idea! She might have lost me, and this caused her never-ending fright.

As is well known, sleepwalkers are agile, and they are protected by some supernatural force. If you ever have to deal with someone in that state, avoid talking loudly or disturbing the person. As you approach a sleepwalker, he or she remains unaware of your presence. Act and intervene with the greatest prudence to avoid injury.

Hunting Crocs, Losing Legs

We are still in the town of Vinh-long about my seventh year. There was no television, and I was too young to have a radio. For a *"bambin"* [rhymes with Chopin], a little boy, days were long. I had toys which managed to distract me, but I was in search of more adventurous undertakings! Luckily there stood that infamous terrace, whence I could observe the goings-on along the Mekong River for hours on end. From up there, as I contemplated my adventures, I watched the indigenous workers. This river surface was lively and bustling, and you heard the high pitched cries of people communicating from one boat to another. The little steamboats slipped along and made their steam whistles heard. You also had the little junks, wooden sailboats with their sails neatly cut in characteristic fashion.

All along the edge of the river you'd see what we called *habitations flottantes*, floating dwellings with roofs made of bamboo and covered with thatch. These boats housed the native people throughout the seasons, and some were even equipped for commerce, since they carried all kinds of products and merchandise. You'd see junks and *habitations flottantes* lined up side by side. At times they were four or five boats deep, creating a contiguous flotilla, starting from the bank and forming a village on water which ran a hundred feet from the shore. To get from a boat to the riverbank, people would jump from one boat to the next.

A bit farther up or downstream there were fishing boats. It was just that the fishermen couldn't use their nets due to the prolific abundance of crocodiles, carnivores that devoured the living things that crossed their paths. They even crawled out of the river at night, onto terra firma, where they snapped up what they could find, be it a chicken, a rabbit or a little pig. If by misfortune any overconfident kids were playing late at night, they risked the same fate.

Speaking of crocs, in those years of 1928 to 1930 or so, it was the supreme statement of high fashion for ladies and gents to have shoes, purses, belts and wallets fashioned out of crocodile hide. Be it known that the meat in that long tail is very tasty too, whether served up as steaks or providing the base for a delicious soup. Well, the problem, then, is how the devil would one capture these reptiles?

Here is a true but incredible story which sticks out in my mind. I was on the terrace when I witnessed a remarkable trick that the natives used, dangerous though it was. I saw a very narrow canoe carrying two natives, crocodile hunters, who were kneeling. The canoe was so skinny and the sides were so low that any little tip would have sent the men into the water. The one in the stern of the boat paddled and steered the team toward the crocodile. He paddled up until the time he took, into one hand, a club which had a mass of wood on the striking end. His other hand steadied the side of the canoe as he awaited the perfect moment to spring into action. The other native, up in the bow, had his leg out dangling in the water... as bait! To myself I thought how "nuts" this guy must be. Well, after all, no: it was a plenty dangerous method but a feasible one. The trick was for these natives to be super quick, because the croc himself certainly was.

All of a sudden, there's a croc! It was swimming toward the leg dangling in the water. The bowman of the canoe, the one with his leg in the water, was holding firmly in one hand a pointed stick. It was about a foot long and sharpened at both ends. As soon as the croc got up near the boat, the native yanked his leg out of the water as he simultaneously poked the two-pointed stick into the open mouth of the croc, the croc with gaping jaws that was preparing to take off that same leg! When his sharp stick had been planted in the animal's mouth, the other man moved forward fast as lightning and clubbed the top of the animal's mouth with that heavy instrument. The two of them pulled the beast into the boat as the one man continued to hammer down with sweeping strokes of his club. The croc twisted and squirmed, almost to the point of capsizing them, but one well placed *coup de grâce* from that club brought calm in the boat.

Our men had their quarry, representing a nice piece of profit for them. Not only had they brought home dinner for many meals, but a crocodile hide did bring a pretty penny on the open market. From time to time we'd meet a poor man in the village streets who had a leg missing. One could wonder if, on one occasion, the croc had been quicker than the man.

Dreaded Spanking Tool: onward toward Manhood

As I reached the age of eight or nine, I started to behave myself better. Plenty of times, though, I'd tease my nanny, enacting some kind of farce on her. This evoked a "*Jacquot, veux-tu te conduire comme il le faut ?*" (Will you conduct yourself properly?) from her. If I happened to push the trick beyond the limits of proper etiquette, and if she considered my actions to be out of place or too bold, I got threatened with being turned over to my father who would surely use the *martinet*. A discipline session with him often involved this implement, a wooden handle which had leather thongs attached to one end. My father placed the greatest of faith in whatever Assam reported to him. Since I was typically dressed in shorts, a whipping with leather strings was something to be avoided! Today I can confirm that often I deserved it. Assam went to my father only on rare occasions when my rascal acts surpassed the limits. Otherwise she simply slapped me with her two characteristic licks, and even then she would feel remorse and would bend over backwards excusing herself. She always had tons of good intentions for her little Jacquot.

My Assam decided I was too big to sit on her lap and go shopping in a one-seat rickshaw, so she started hiring a bigger rickshaw. They had these new models with three wheels, and to this day I wonder how in the world the poor driver could handle that thing. This modern innovation came to be called a *cyclo* [pronounce see-CLO], having a seat and a set of pedals which the brave chauffeur set himself to turning for all he was worth. I recall thinking to myself how both this *cyclo* and the regular rickshaw called a *pousse-pousse* [pronounce pooss-pooss, literally meaning "push-push"] must have been exhausting work. Generally the *cyclo* was used for longer distances, when its speed had a true advantage, and it did cost a bit more.

Going to the park often called for a *cyclo*. Several nannies in our part of town would set a time to meet up, taking multiple *cyclos*, each being designed to carry two adults. Seeing as how these nannies loved to gossip, they tended to poke the kids into *cyclos* of their own, allowing the nannies more opportunity to talk. Off we'd go, either side by side or one *cyclo* following the other, but this was not always the best of ideas. Just like kids of all eras and all places, we fought among ourselves and hollered. For a time, nannies would lose control. At some point, though, peace and calm inevitably returned.

I sit here recalling the episode of Marie Rose, a little friend of my own age, and a bit of a flirt she was. One time in the *cyclo* she was playing with "things" beyond the limits of protocol, albeit purely out of curiosity and not out of vice. Boys were different from girls, and she simply had to verify this. It only brought laughter from our nannies, who realized our childish innocence and didn't fret over it.

At the park, by contrast, we'd drive the nannies crazy as we played hide-and-go-seek in the bushes, among the bigger trees and around the corners of buildings. The nannies knew that when we were out of sight for too long we were likely to start some mischief, and these mischievous acts were indeed a cause for concern.

All in all, a healthy growing boy who develops normally will indeed develop curiosity. My nanny picked up on it just as did my folks. In my era, sexual innocence extended to age thirteen, fourteen, even fifteen, unlike the modern era. Nowadays, sex is an open topic, even in schools, from a young age.

As for me, at school, my academic performance was far from satisfactory. This caused my parents to become troubled, especially my father. He was outraged that my spoken Annamite was better than my French. A certain tolerance on his part turned into grand exasperation. As soon as he became acutely aware that I was two years behind the usual program, he decided to take the matter firmly into his own hands.

War Pilot Memoirs: A Mirror on 1939

CHAPTER 2

My Youth: Pre-War Paris, 1930s

Patriarchal Decision: France

My father decided that the time to take action had arrived. It would soon befall me to see my world turned upside down, to leave my sweet Orient behind, this peaceful colonial existence. Papa wanted me to face up to reality; he wanted me to become a responsible adult. It caught me off guard. I was to be cut off from my nanny whom I adored, because his decision was to send me to France for more serious academic work. My mother was to travel to France anyway in that year of 1932 for six months or so. This was for her health, in the form of a visit to the therapeutic baths, and for her mental wellbeing to revisit life on the home front.

So I went with my mother in all confidence that nothing bad lay before me. The surprise sprang up in my path there at the gates of Moreau School at Choisy-le-Roy in the suburbs of Paris. It was a private school, all boys, and immense. It was one of those finishing schools designed for families who wanted their boys to have a proper education. The boarding school setup, or *pension complète* whereby we lived and ate on campus, included activities in the gym and in the swimming pool. Surrounding the whole place was a brick wall, both tall and thick, and there were metal pickets everywhere making me think of prison. Our professors were strict, and we were watched day and night by monitors. Needless to say, I had a heavy heart, but I think it was even worse for my mother. Separating from her only child and leaving him in the hands of these monsters? At the end of six months, it was surely with great difficulty that she went back to Saigon, leaving me alone in Paris.

My father had instilled in me the concept that it was all up to me. He had said, "If you work hard, if you make up the lost time, you will be compensated." Soon enough I figured out that this compensation would be monetary, and his checks were indeed copious. This gave me strength, and I quickly retook the proper road.

During these three difficult years I managed to complete my Middle School Certificate (*certificat d'études primaires*) and my Commercial Diploma (*diplôme commercial*). Even though all seemed to be going ok, I came to know during this time a grand sadness which infiltrates a young man's soul, a sadness at being far removed from family. It's difficult for a young man about age ten or twelve to comprehend the wisdom in a good decision on the part of adults to whom he is beloved. Because of my good schoolwork and the fact that my parents came to realize how miserable I was, they eventually made arrangements with one of my aunts, a Parisian, to replace Assam in overseeing my development.

Assam

Before moving away from that most crucial period of a young man's life, I simply must discuss my nanny and nurse and tutor in greater detail. When Assam's services were terminated, she returned to Hong Kong, her native city. Assam was from a well-established Chinese family that, from generation to generation, specialized in care-giving for European children. These nurse-maids or nannies had to complete special schooling for this. Extremely devoted, each one of them became a second mother to a child. The biological mother granted the most extreme confidence, not only for pedagogical expertise but also for medical knowl-

CHAPTER 2 *My Youth: Pre-War Paris, 1930s*

edge. My Assam was the most patient of the patient, with an easygoing nature, and she was always in good spirits. Her French was very good. Her wearing apparel was always impeccable, generally a white, Chinese style blouse buttoned straight up to the neckline, and a black taffeta pair of pants. Her hairstyle was simple, her pitch-black hair pulled back into a little knot. Her footwear was multicolor sandals decorated with needlepoint and colored beads.

Every morning she was in the habit of consulting my mother to lay out the day's agenda. This way Assam could organize things and make the most benefit of the day. I was entirely in Assam's care, and she supervised my hygiene: bath or shower, brushing teeth and combing hair. It was she who picked out my clothes based on the day's activities. She repaired my clothes when they got torn or dirty, and luckily she was really good at this. She taught me to speak Cantonese, as opposed to Mandarin which she said was more difficult and was used more for writing. She was the shadow of my guardian angel both day and night.

Anytime the family went traveling, Assam traveled too. There was never any question that things be otherwise, and Father had to travel often. When the family would be in France, Assam was a central focus of curiosity. Fortunately she was not bothered by this and loved to accompany my mother for the shopping. Often Assam wound up going to the butcher's shop or the little grocer's by herself. She was welcomed by them, since Assam knew how to make herself liked by everybody. She'd strike up conversations with the clerks, whether guys or girls, and she'd make small talk over the differences of French life to what she'd known in China.

In Paris: a new *Tutrice* (not a Nursemaid, not a Tutor, but a "*Tutrice*")

Here I was at age thirteen, in a boarding school, and without my Assam! My parents had decided I needed a *tutrice*, a person to oversee both my personal life and my school life, and of course

I needed one in Paris. The logical choice was my mother's younger sister, Betty. She was married to Uncle Leon Nant who ran the Colonial-European Enterprise of Import Export (*Agence Coloniale et Européene d'Importation et Exportation*) which traded food products and other goods. Their apartment was way up on the ninth floor, located in arrondissement number eighteen in Paris, on a street called "rue du Général de Maud'huy." They also maintained a home in Saigon, containing an office for my uncle who had to travel very much. While he and my aunt would be away, there was Tino, my uncle's sister, who lived in the same apartment.

My parents decided that I could share the apartment with Tino, which I viewed as a benediction from God. She was a delightful person, and she liked me a lot. An unmarried woman, gifted with a surprising musical talent, she was a violinist and sat second chair in the orchestra of the Musical Conservatory at *l'Opéra de Paris*, yet she'd decided not to make this a career.

*   *   *

Oh, I was happy when the day came that studies at Choisy-le-Roy were over and done with. My father had decided that I would become an engineer, so here I was, age fourteen, enrolled in a school there in Paris called Breguet Falguières, being told to study Mechanical and Electrical Engineering for the next five years. It was 1936. The good news was that this school did not house any students on campus. Via public bus, I commuted from and to the apartment. I had become a studious little devil. Since I was a lover of graphic arts, I got myself enrolled also at Beaux Arts for night school, but since my parents would have disapproved, I did this in secret. Tino was "in" on my little plot and agreed that I should hide this from my parents. These extra studies put me late getting back to the apartment, but Tino covered for me. I swore to her never to get in past eleven o'clock pm, and I really had no desire to go roaming the streets anyway. I had promised, and that was that.

In 1937 at age fifteen I passed my tests which gave me a degree called *brevet élémentaire* from this Engineering school. My father kept his word, and monetary gifts followed. It was our intention to see me get the *brevet supérieur* in 1940. I was in a happy state: with this money I could pay for my night classes at the art academy. Hmm, but this was without his knowing.

My Emancipation

Admittedly by the age of fifteen my sexual yearnings were taking hold, and Tino picked up on this. How could she not? She was the one who did my laundry. Sharing common ground and many relaxed conversations with Tino, it bears noting that she was remarkably well-informed for a single gal, many of her opinions being both definitive and well founded. I felt at ease with this sister to my uncle by marriage and we had no trouble discussing these rather personal subjects.

Every Saturday morning I used to go to the public swimming pool. In a polite, gentle way, Tino said to me, "You ought to take along some money, just in case you meet a nice girl."

I stared right back at her in surprise, with, "Why, Tino, do you conjure up such an event?"

"Oh, I don't know," she said. "It's just a little instinct I have. Besides, you are working too hard. With all your studies and different sports, dedicate a little time to leisure. A nice young girl with some worldly knowledge could show you the things you're missing out on. This might avoid some embarrassing mistakes in the future."

A little perturbed, naively I said, "Like what?"

Ever so politely, she came back with, "But, Jacquot, just the idea of, for example, getting a girl pregnant. I don't think your parents would like that at all. They'd crucify you!"

A short silence followed. With a smirk on my face, taking her under my arm, I told her, "Oh, but Tino, you're going to teach me all I have to know about that!"

She laughed lightly as she pinched my cheek, and said, "Listen, young stud-muffin, I'm a bit too old for those things. *Allez*, get out of here. Go to Pigalle Square. That's where you'll find women to teach you this stuff, and for goodness' sake pick a pretty one. Ha."

Pigalle Square, Paris, a part of town well known for its cabarets where bodacious singers performed suggestive songs, is nowadays where you'd find pornographic bookstores and prostitutes working the sidewalks. For a sexual rendezvous, most hotels offered acceptance. Nonetheless, the world famous Moulin Rouge was nearby with its French Cancan, and just adjacent to Pigalle Square sat Montmartre where anybody could watch the artists at work in the open air, under parasols or just under the trees.

Getting back to Tino's suggestion, it sort of left me confused, but I said to myself, "Why not?" The weather was hot that day. I got off the public bus at the Pigalle bus stop and, just to quench my thirst, I entered a bistro to get a nice cold beer. The bistro was filled to capacity. I noticed a lot of women: young, not so young, pretty girls and some that you might call unattractive. They seemed to be wearing just a bit too much makeup and skirts that were kind of short, and there weren't many guys. I was discovering a new world, a facet of human existence which was unfamiliar to me.

I developed a sensation of anxiety, so I drank my beer quickly in preparation for getting the heck out of there. I stood up, but in order to exit I would have to squeeze past the edge of a table where a pretty blonde was seated alone. She was not at all like the others, since she was tastefully dressed, wearing less makeup and she had matching purse and shoes. There was a glass of something on the table. As I passed her table, she got up with a handsome smile and said, "Excuse me. Maybe you can help me. There's a problem with my car. I can't get it started. Do you know something about cars?"

Not recognizing this as part of a feminine ruse, I responded as

CHAPTER 2   *My Youth: Pre-War Paris, 1930s*

a good Samaritan should, "Sure. Where's your car?" Even out of the corner of my eye she seemed very attractive.

She picked up her handbag and we walked out together. It did seem a bit odd, especially now with the other women in the place calling out, "Eh, Nadine, you're taking 'em from the cradle, huh? Don't forget his little bib."

I looked at her, saying, "So, your name is Nadine?"

All smiles, she replied, "Yes. What's yours? And don't pay any attention to those girls. They are *professionnelles*."

"How do you know them?" I asked.

"Oh, I'm a regular at this bistro, so they kind of know me and we talk."

I had no call to be suspicious of her also being a "professional." Her way of carrying herself was different. She was dressed in a simpler, more charming style, and she had something about her that rendered her respectfully desirable. We got to her car, a little Simca, and I opened the hood. I looked around the motor while she tried starting it. It didn't start, but during my examination I noticed a spark plug wire dangling which should have been attached. I squeezed it on firmly and had her try again. Bravo. Running!

She thanked me, saying, "Let me buy you a drink."

"Oh, no," I responded. "I'm a little late already. I'd better get going."

She said, "Can we get together somehow? Since I owe you for the service, at least I'll have the chance to offer you a drink. We can get to know each other. Here's my phone number. Let's make it next Saturday, at the Café Chez Martin near the Notre Dame metro entrance, at about 6pm?"

I gave my ok, and off rolled Nadine in her Simca as she waved goodbye.

When I got back to the apartment I was happy as a lark. To Tino I recounted my little adventure. "Well, how did it turn out?" said Tino.

"Great," I said. "We got along fine and we set a rendezvous for next Saturday."

Tino, with her little snicker of a smile, said, "So you put it off for a week, huh?"

That evening at dinner I was still beside myself, and I explained to Tino how fast the day had gone by, the vision of this charming girl's face in my mind. I felt, within me, a sense of well-being surrounding this "Episode of Nadine."

The Rendezvous

When Saturday finally came, I was faithful to the appointed hour. I was pleased to see her on time and wearing a tight-fitting little skirt. She had let her hair down, so now her long blond hair fell to the middle of her back and this made her even more alluring. She was wearing a tight sweater which really, shall we say, validated her bosom. We chatted for the longest time, as she told me of her family, her parents being middleclass residents of the outskirts of Paris. She had two younger sisters and she herself was age twenty-two. She worked as a retail clerk in the shopping district Galleries Lafayette and lived alone in a studio apartment. Now she abruptly asked me how old I was. Yikes, I revealed my young age. Lifting her eyebrow, she said, "You seem older than that, but you are a minor. I wonder if I should avoid taking you to my place."

I, in turn, knitted my brow, and just like a big dummy I said, "What do you mean, 'minor'?" She figured out that I was not up to speed, that I had not figured out she was a *fille de joie* [literally "girl of joy"]. She took my hand in hers, stared straight into my eyes, and said nothing. I was the one who reacted, saying, "No, it cannot be."

"Oh yes," she said. "I find myself in a different set of circumstances from the rest, but nevertheless I have to practice this profession." I was dumbfounded.

"I'll tell you the circumstances, Jacques, and then you can decide what you want to do." She, in a very simple fashion and without false modesty, explained the reasons behind what she did. Being from a good family, she had not suspected anything that day when, with some friends, she'd been in a bar yet without knowing there were prostitutes in the bar. (In 1937, prostitution was allowed in Paris under government control.) It was bad luck, then, that even into this bar of good reputation there arrived some officers, a sort of Vice Squad or Morals Police. They rounded up the prostitutes and put them all into a paddy-wagon, and Nadine got included. Poor Nadine was caught off guard and did not know why she, too, got carted off. Unjust as it seemed, they treated her just like all the true prostitutes. She was given a control number, and a little card, and from then on she had to undergo a medical examination every week. Also required was a report to this Morals Police on her activities.

Apparently, once you got caught just one time, you could have your card and control number erased only by paying a sizable sum of money, and Nadine did not have it. She had never had the guts to present the problem to her parents, so here she sat, in this predicament. Telling me the story, I noticed tears in her eyes. Then she said to me, "So you see why I cannot pursue any affair with you. You are too young. They could put me in jail."

I found her way of coping with the circumstances to be very noble. She possessed a good sense of duty, and she revealed by her manners a good education. Having listened to her story, I made the decision to get myself invited to her apartment. I found her to be sincere, and I chose to have faith in her. Well, too, I must admit I found her very, very attractive. Without further ado, we agreed. She liked my idea of going up to her place and admitted to having an attraction for me also. Need I spell it out? For the next two years we met up frequently, right up until the time the war came down on us all.

Seven long years would have come and gone when, in vain, I tried to find Nadine in post-war Paris. Out of curiosity, I wanted to know what might have become of her, what had gone on during the German occupation of Paris, and if her family might have re-established ties with her. Sadly, and not relaying much detail, neighbors told me she had been shot to death, having been routed out in a mass raid by the Germans. This impacted me gravely, since it hurt to think of such a kind and generous girl dying that way. She had found a special place in my heart, since it truly was she who turned a boy into a man.

*   *   *

Of all the sports I enjoyed, Judo was one I picked up again there in Paris of the 1930s, and I worked out at the Judo Club for many years. I had studied Judo from age six back in Indochina. At the Breguet school there was an excellent sports center set up for everything from soccer to javelin to the shot put. I applied myself well to this field of human endeavor and I got pretty good. Then, wow: I discovered fencing. The *fleuret* and the saber became my passion as I really excelled in this sport. I felt sure I had been a pirate in some previous life, on the deck of some galleon at war, in the era of Cardinal Richelieu.

En Garde! True Duel for Love

One swashbuckler of a story comes to mind. Two or three friends at the Breguet school shared my passion for this sport. My best friend, André, was truly gifted. André and I used to go out trying to pick up girls near the woods called Bois de Boulogne just west of Paris. Of course, at age fifteen the male animal is invincible, and, in his own eyes, very special in the world. We took many things too seriously and had very little perspective on reality. Among buddies, it was common to quarrel over a girl. I recall a charming girl of good upbringing named Josette, and she and I got along really well. André had his eye on her too. Truth be told, I think Josette was feigning the innocent role as she played us for puppets one against the other. Playing the possessive puppet, I became jealous. André and I decided to fight a duel, and the winner would take Josette. Imagine, if you will, these two brainless wonders, both age fifteen, who thought themselves to be so crafty.

CHAPTER 2 *My Youth: Pre-War Paris, 1930s*

In a proper training environment you put on masks, padded uniforms and gloves for a duel. Each guy would pick out an epee, having a squared-off tip to prevent injury. Just like wild bull elephants on a rampage, having lost all power of reason, off we went. We had no protective gear, and we had broken off the square tips of the epees to make things real! We located an empty field for this duel, *à la d'Artagnan*. We were both adept with epees, so suddenly and simultaneously the tips of our epees found the flesh of the wrist and dug in, wounding both of us. Blood flowed. We screamed. Throwing our epees to the ground, we squeezed upon our wrists to slow down the blood flow. Luckily the injuries were minimal, and there was no nerve damage. We stared at each other, wide-eyed. Realizing how idiotic this was, we made up with a bear hug. All our animosity gone, we said, roughly in unison, "To the devil with Josette."

Now we needed to get treatment for our wounds, but there would be explanations to make at home. "How did this happen, poor boy?" Back at the apartment, I worked Tino in this way: playing soccer in a field where there was a bunch of debris, including a certain broken bottle, I'd had the misfortune of playing goalie and having to dive for a save. Tino looked at me in such a way as to communicate that she was swallowing, at most, half of my story. She led me into the bathroom where the first aid box was. Politely she said, "There's only one good remedy, but it's gonna hurt. We need to staple the wound." Quickly planned, quickly done.

The bandage in place, she said, "I don't know how on Earth that thing penetrated so deep." I never did admit to her what had happened, but I certainly practiced fencing with a whole new set of values.

Bows & Arrows with Pre-War NAZIs

I got back into archery too, having started this at a young age, just like Judo. I participated in many competitions and was awarded a National Medal in archery. My bow was a flat flanged aluminum bow, made in England, and the upper and lower halves were precision-fitted where they joined to form the grip. The pull was forty-five pounds. For a target fifty yards away, you had to shoot upward at a pretty steep angle, so you had to bear in mind the wind which took the arrow off course. To win the championship, you had to hit the center of the target at fifty yards, the size of which looked like a dime when you hold the coin at full arm's length.

The red of the target was in truth the size of a dinner plate, but I had a secret advantage. As a little boy in Indochina, I had been blessed with learning to shoot from the Moï tribe. My uncle owned a rubber plantation where the whole tribe worked, harvesting sap from his rubber trees. On weekends I used to accompany my uncle to the plantation where I could mingle with these workers, who were very excellent archers. They taught me archery in the wild, and I carried those little tricks in my head. The Moïs also taught me how to use the fascinating weapon called a *sarbacane*, or blowgun, which they used to hunt little animals and birds.

I remember it was in the stadium, in the archery section, where my instructor came to me saying there was a German team, young students, who wanted to see how we French measured up. He told me, "I'm sending you and one other contestant to compete with them. You're going to Cologne!"

*   *   *

I felt very honored, and happy to get to go to Germany, as this was my first trip to that country. On the other hand, you should know that Nazism was already in full vigor. You saw the swastika, the cross with arms shaped like a capital letter gamma in Greek, on all the flags and on many armbands of young people in uniform. The air was heavy. This Germanic mentality that pervaded the atmosphere is hard to express in words, but it was arrogant. You already could feel their stares upon you which made you uncomfortable. The common will, the common mission, was to demonstrate that we foreigners were of a race inferior to theirs.

CHAPTER 2 *My Youth: Pre-War Paris, 1930s*

It was really incredible.

Ten targets were set up in the stadium where we were to compete. A group of young German contestants was already in place, all in black uniforms, and all wearing armbands on the left arm which touted that dreaded swastika. We were positioned French, German, French, German, each with his own target out there in front of him. Vividly I remember the guy next to me, Fritz, looking at me out of the corner of his eye. In a substandard French, with an arrogant grin, he said to me, "You get not chance of winning. We to be stronger."

Over the loudspeaker we heard the announcement to get set. Each of us had eight arrows, and for first place you had to put five of them into the red center. Five in the red got you a gold medal, four, a silver, and three, a bronze. There was a huge crowd. Before we could start the tournament we had not only to listen to the national anthem, but we had to be respectful and salute.

The tournament began. I shot, and by just an inch I missed the red part. Our young Fritz missed it too, then he looked at me smiling to say, "I let you go easy this time. You have hope this way." I shot again. I missed: too low. Our wily Fritz shot. He scored a red. He rejoiced, all the while watching me out of the corner of his eye. Again I launched my arrow, which fell right on the line between red and white. Oh, darn the luck, it didn't count. Fritz went again: another red. I groaned, and my heart beat faster. There were five arrows left. Controlling my breathing, taking my time, I shot. Finally I had a red. Our friend Fritz never got any more reds after his first two. Suddenly the wind came up and this made me nervous, but despite it all I obtained a bronze medal with three arrows in the red.

It was now my turn to look at Fritz and, with a chuckle, to say to him, "Maybe you had a piece of straw in your eye. What a shame."

Fritz took it hard and showed his rage. Hand on his dagger, which so many of the young Nazis carried, with a pompous air, he said, "We will see. Soon will we know what winner is." He spat on the ground, then off he went. Fast as we could, our team beat it back to France, wanting to get out of this country, so unfriendly even then.

With reverence I have safely kept that bow all these years. It's now a collectors' item. They don't make that style anymore.

In 1938, personally I was not fully convinced that the Germans envisioned a global war, especially since Neville Chamberlain, the British Prime Minister, was denying it as well. We were being told that Germany was simply "on practice maneuvers." Yet why, and against whom? You could already feel an unhealthy wind blowing within that country.

*   *   *

Now it was summer vacation, 1938, and I had just turned sixteen. Happy as could be, I got invited by Aunt Lucie, actually a distant cousin to Papa, to visit her near Royan. This town is on the west coast of France, on the Atlantic, and it's in a region frequented for vacations, even therapeutic vacations given its good salt air. There was a white sand beach two miles long. This town was a good example of 1930s architecture and culture, and most of the homes of this era were very pretty. Architects were meticulous with details. The bricks were red, the roofs were red, and frescos were painted around doorways and windows. Nearby Meschers-les-Bains was the site of a famous casino.

This beach had the shape of a long drawn-out horseshoe. On the left end you saw Valière Point, and on the right, *Pointe des blagueurs* or Jokers' Point. The distance over water between the two was almost three miles. Currents were strong. Since I was a good distance swimmer, I made this swim plenty of times, sometimes finding myself faced with contrary wind and current. The strength of the current overwhelmed me at times, but, determined little booger that I was, it simply took a little more time to get from point to point. My cousins, with less fortitude, declined to join me, so I swam it alone, while they carried my clothes around to the far side and waited. A few times, I think they got worried whether I would make it across or not.

CHAPTER 2   *My Youth: Pre-War Paris, 1930s*   33

Aunt Lucie's house was located right next to a large natural gas storage tank and its gas meter. Many times bigger than the house, this gas tank serviced the city of Royan. Her house was neatly adorned with a gorgeous yard, full of apple trees, peach trees and of course a multitude of flowers. This setting gave the house a sumptuous feel, an impression of easy living. This particular summer I was with cousin Henri, my age, and cousin Françoise was there, but she was a lot younger at age eight. It was a 15-minute walk from the house to the beach, so my cousins and I went to the beach every day. We went unsupervised, since the adults had faith in us. I made a lot of friends, and all of them were just like us and loved to play out on the beach. We experienced the bliss of childhood, talking amongst ourselves and doing a lot of "stuff." We'd take long walks to explore the oceanfront, and there were vendors galore so we could buy nifty things, including food. Cooking aromas tickled our nostrils, like sugar-waffles, berlingozzo candies (the ones shaped into four triangular sides), little pink shrimp, French fried potatoes, ice cream... oh, what a memory.

Aunt Lucie's house was big, and her bedroom was upstairs while we kids shared one on the first floor. She gave me the responsibility, during the day, of watching out for my cousins. At age sixteen I guess she trusted me. Our jaunts were frequent but short-lived, since Aunt Lucie liked to know where we were and what we were up to. Many a time she'd come looking for us, but always with a cake or pie or some kind of ice cream. On certain occasions I was allowed to go meet up with my own pals, some of whom were older than me, and we'd do some ocean swimming or just talk.

One day we found out that a troupe of actors was in the area. They were there to film a movie with Danielle Darrieux, who was a well known star. I really liked her. Armand Bernard, Elvire Popesco and others were there too, and they had set up headquarters near the casino. The name of the movie was *La belle Bordelaise* and Danielle Darrieux was the leading lady; she actually was "Bordelaise", born in the city of Bordeaux. When the day was through, you could find all the actors in the casino, seeking distraction. There was a stage band playing outdoors so they could dance in the open air on a smooth, tile floor. I loved to dance, and in my family this came naturally. I would have loved to infiltrate this group of actors, but there was a security force that kept nonmembers of the troupe away from the dance floor. Notwithstanding my age of sixteen, I looked eighteen. Possessing plenty of testicular fortitude, I would gladly have tried, but for the moment I held back.

There was a problem to overcome: Aunt Lucie always sent us to bed at nine o'clock, so how could I get away? She rode herd in a very strict way on this matter, and I thought her to be overbearing. Of course, I wanted to go dancing. Then the courage came to me: it was after nine o'clock, all was calm, a gentle breeze was coming through the open window, the cousins were whispering to avoid disturbing Aunt Lucie who was upstairs snoring like a locomotive anyway, so I slipped on some appropriate clothes. Donning a nice shirt and necktie, I gave the shush sign to my cousins, whispering, "You've seen nothing, heard nothing, got it?" I slipped out the window which opened directly onto the street where the big gas reservoir was. Slick and quick and silent, I boogied down the road toward the casino. It took fifteen minutes to get there, and of course my heart was racing when I arrived.

Even from far off I could hear the stage band playing, but now there I was right behind the casino, which faced the beach. The band was jammin', twenty or so musicians in neat rows on an elevated pedestal. There were tables and chairs strewn hither and thither around the band, and I noticed curiosity-seekers all over the place. There stood a group of my friends, watching the movie stars dancing. There was a lot of noise: singing, laughing, everybody drinking, everybody partying.

I made it over to where my buddies were. We were laughing and joking, all in good fun, and someone came up with a challenge, a bet. Wagering a good chunk of money, the bet was that I go invite Danielle Darrieux to the dance floor! Huh? These guys were almost bound to win since there was a security force to be gotten through, keeping not only kids away but keeping everybody away. Yikes, even if I did get through, I'd never have the guts to take her in my arms. The truth is, I was told later on, that Danielle Darrieux had quite the reputation for liking young guys.

What a challenge, but let's just say my buddies didn't know me very well. I put my brain into gear, trying to find a trick. Success was imperative. The worst that could happen would be getting stopped by the security guys. It was a mellow evening, and I could tell the film crew had imbibed plenty. Security seemed "down" a bit, kind of relaxed. I found a course of action: I wiggled my way in among the cinematic troupe. Danielle was just finishing up on the dance floor and her partner had already disappeared. After a momentary break, the band struck up a Tango.

I picked up on the fact that Danielle was all by herself, but, jeesh, surely just for a second or two. She was all smiles. She was smoothing her dress. Then, johnny-on-the-spot, I stepped over with the most charming smile in my arsenal, and I took her in my arms. Wow, there we were, arms intertwined, actually on the dance floor! She was dancing, with a surprised demeanor, but dancing just the same. She gave me a "*Qui es-tu ?*" ("Who are you?"). A sensation of redness in my face came over me, but I continued dancing.

Quickly I said to her, "Please, for goodness' sake, keep dancing. Help me. The guys made a bet that I didn't have the guts to dance with you." She was amused, very amused.

She looked me straight in the face, then scanned me from head to toe, before saying, "You dance very well, and I think you're nice."* Bingo! I had won the bet. We kept on for two more dances, then she wanted to get back to her table where there stood a very elegant gentleman. She presented me to him, Henri Decoin, the Executive Producer, her <u>husband</u>. I felt as if I'd melted on the floor.

* "You're not bad," translates the « *T'es pas mal* » which Jacques shared with me over a drink. JH

At the next table, she introduced me to her brother who was my own age. Politely, he invited me to join him at his table as Danielle went back to the dance floor with her husband. Danielle's brother wasn't in the movies. He told me that his parents had a house five miles from the casino. He lived there with them, and I presume they were Danielle's parents too. He and I became friends, a good thing since he was a student at the Sorbonne in Paris, and later on we got together often.

Yikes! I looked at my watch, and it was one o'clock in the morning. Time flies when you're having fun. Having pocketed my winnings which tallied a good fifty bucks (my buddies were really blown away by this and had a hard time getting over it), I made haste to get my butt home. Softly, I slipped through the window, and the house still seemed calm. Aunt Lucie, the locomotive, was still snoring, and all the little cousins were asleep. Rapidly I undressed and dove under the covers. The next morning, the whole crowd was assembled for breakfast when Aunt Lucie mentioned she had gotten up in the night for a glass of water. What had occurred? Had she looked in on me? Or perhaps my camouflage was well enough laid out that she hadn't noticed anything and she'd simply gone on back to bed? We will never know.

That producer Henri Decoin was, I think, her first husband. In the year that I'm composing this, Danielle Darrieux is still alive at about age eighty-eight, and I'm aware of stories of, oh, four husbands or so. I've never seen her again except on the silver screen, and I particularly loved *Le bois sacré*, The Sacred Forest.

CHAPTER 2 *My Youth: Pre-War Paris, 1930s*

Nadine, first date

War Pilot Memoirs: A Mirror on 1939

CHAPTER 3

War Breaks: 1940, I am Seventeen

My best friend, a guy from Breguet School, invited me for what would turn out to be the last time I'd vacation in France, for many decades anyway. He invited me for two weeks at his parents' home in the city of Strasbourg on the French side of the Rhine River, facing the Black Forest on the German side. That irritating atmosphere surrounding the German situation was becoming cold, hard problems. It would surely prove to be a westward occupation: France plus Great Britain, and the U.S. would be Hitler's next target according to evidence* discovered years later. It bears mentioning that Denmark, Norway, Sweden and Finland were early battlegrounds with very significant naval and air battles. Hundreds of thousands of future freedom-fighters would go out via the northern French port of Dunkirk, bound for England. Early 1940: we French felt defeated already.

When I got the invitation to vacation in Strasbourg, just a few miles from the German border which at that point is the Rhine, I was seventeen and a half years old. A vacation in Strasbourg suited me fine since it was an unfamiliar part of France for me. My stomping ground was Paris, plus western France around Aunt

---

* diary (March 8, 1940) of U.S. Undersecretary of the Interior Ickes, dining in Washington with Archduke Otto von Hapsburg

Lucie's. My buddy had organized an exciting itinerary of hunting game in the woods, quail and partridges I think it was, plus this was the season for the official Fair and Feast. I was sure we'd spend some quality time together, he and I.

When we boarded the train in Paris bound for Strasbourg, all the trains were filled with soldiers, some young, some not so young. Somebody told me these poor devils were destined for the front lines to defend the country. Did these guys count on coming back alive?

With an almost festive tone, our first week rolled right by. People there seemed to possess a village mentality for this annual celebration, yet my friend, who was from Strasbourg, pointed out to me how the German airplanes were constantly flying over. We noted the lack of any French equivalent in the air.

Our vacation time was not yet over when, one morning, as we nonchalantly strolled past the sports center, the radio was announcing that there was to be a universal conscription for military service. Vividly I recall that radio sitting on the table and how the music got interrupted for the announcement. It was the French Prime Minister, and my memory is clear that it was Mr. Édouard Daladier, who left that office on Wednesday, March 20, 1940, although he served in the succeeding Reynaud government too. He announced that every male having reached his eighteenth birthday was to report immediately for enlistment. I can still picture the loudspeakers, mounted at every street corner in Strasbourg, announcing the German invasion. These loudspeakers, in addition, were giving instructions to the French people. My friend and I experienced mixed emotions: angry to be left out, yet relieved not to be called upon for this appalling duty. We were age seventeen and a half, and the announcements were saying eighteen. With heavy hearts, we watched train stations fill up with soldiers being mobilized. There were so many trains, carrying both troops and weapons, that they seemed to be backed up on the tracks.

A new message came over the loudspeakers: "Young

CHAPTER 3 *War Breaks: 1940, I am Seventeen*

volunteers needed, for supervising children to be transported to Paris." What a godsend. I had to get back to Paris anyway, in fact it was a number one priority, so I was one of the first in line to sign up for this mission. Identification tags, giving name, age and address, were strung around the necks of all the little kids. My suitcase in hand, and with the same kind of nametag pinned to my jacket, I walked into the train station. What a mass of confusion! There was crying, screaming and the hollering of orders. Everybody was crawling all over everybody, and this in the midst of loudspeaker sirens and locomotive engines which were squealing.

German Stukas Attack

While we monitors assembled the kids, there were workers up on the roof of the train with red paint which was followed by white paint as they blanketed us with the Red Cross symbol. I took this to indicate these train cars contained noncombatants. Society was in chaos; nothing worked anymore. There was no phone service, stores were closing left and right, and overhead there was that infernal drone of aircraft.

We had just learned about a Stuka attack on a regular train, without any Red Cross, just an hour before. This "Dive Combat Airplane" was a long German word* abbreviated "Stuka" and it was known for its Jericho Trumpet, a wailing siren. I felt a bit anxious until I rationalized: we have crosses painted on our train cars.

Off we went. The kids were plenty jumpy, but the older ones helped calm the younger ones down, as the ages ranged from six to twelve. In my compartment of seven feet wide by nine feet long we had fifteen kids stacked up, crying for their parents, and I had to impose a bit of order into this chaos. My duty was to see them to Paris, intact, in a condition of security as best I could provide. We were westbound, with one hour of tracks behind us, yet we didn't really know how much time reaching Paris would

---

* *Sturzkampfflugzeug* = Dive Combat Airplane

take. There were many stops and predictably some bottlenecks ahead of us.

After a brief stop, we had just pulled out when, to my horror, I saw explosions on the ground around us! Our train car was shaking violently, since there were German planes in the air attacking the train. All my kids started screaming: some of them crying, some shrieking. I formed a covey of children under my arms to the best of my ability, trying to reassure them. A little girl about age five hid her head in my jacket. Despite the bombs dropped from the planes, the train continued on. The noise was like the amplified sound of cracking chestnuts. Oh, my God, there were machinegun bullets raining down everywhere. To myself I was thinking why, oh why would these Krauts ignore the Red Cross emblems? We should be shielded, protected. What about the Geneva Convention? These Germans were devoid of respect! Lots of kids got injured. There on my left I saw a young boy who was bleeding but no longer moving. He was dead.

I cried. "This cannot be," I shrieked to the heavens. "Oh, you bastards," I screamed at them. My blood boiling, I truly saw red as I swore to avenge these children someday.

As the train regained its usual speed, the machinegun fire seemed to have stopped, and that predictable period of shock and calm descended. At the next station, we pulled in so they could unload the wounded kids into ambulances, and so they could remove the dead. Those who were lightly wounded were placed in the care of the Red Cross. We took on food and supplies, then the train pulled out in haste so as to avoid risking another attack.

We made it into Paris, the North Station. I remember hearing how there was a lot of activity in and around the country of Belgium as these events unfolded. The Germans would go right around the Maginot Line [pronounce mah-zjee-NOH], those complex underground installations on our eastern front, using Belgium as an end-around maneuver. They would perform lightning warfare in our country, their well-known Blitzkrieg... well, now it's known.

CHAPTER 3 *War Breaks: 1940, I am Seventeen* 43

Once I was in Paris, I made a beeline for the closest Recruitment Center to sign up to serve in the Air Corps. I was madder than hell over what I had been through in the preceding hours. I wanted to become a fighter pilot! The only mission visible before my eyes was to engage these German barbarians <u>as quickly as possible</u>. To my great disappointment, they turned me down. I was flabbergasted over how they insisted on eighteen years on the button, when here I was at seventeen years and about ten months.

I headed back home with a torment in my brain. I told Tino about the events on the train from Strasbourg and about how the recruiters refused to take me into the Air Corps. Calmly she said to me, "Go try another recruitment center. You never know. Maybe some other officer will take you in." Tino was wholeheartedly in favor of my decision to join, and I recall how she said, "If those bloody Krauts come into Paris...." Well, she was ready to defend herself, too.

Tino, in the years 1943 and 44, would take part in the *Résistance*, the French Interior Forces. Her name is printed in the Gold Book, the registry of the freedom fighters whom we call *maquisards* [pronounce mah-kee-ZAHR]. In the alphabetical section, "N" starts with: *NANT, née HECQUET-CHATEL Berthe, Paris; NANT, Tino*. "Berthe" was my Aunt Betty.

As an accomplished alumnus of Fine Arts school, of *Beaux Arts*, I knew I could pull off falsifying a birth record! The need had arisen, so no sooner said than done. I simply changed the "1922" year that was printed, and I must have done a good job since they took me. I was told to be at the Gare de Lyon station the next morning. They boarded us on a train bound for Tours, in central France, 150 miles southwest of Paris, and in my compartment all the guys were really young. Each one had his own story to tell. We shared our thoughts: the why, the how we had come to be there. I recounted that which was still ever so vivid in my mind, the massacre of the innocent children. Squeezing my hands into fists, I pointed them at the sky with the words, "We'll meet again, and you'll pay dearly!"*

* *« On va se rencontrer, et vous allez le payer bien cher »*.

Boot Camp near the City of Tours

Here we were, just arriving at the military base called Meucon [pronounce meuh-KÕ where Õ rhymes with the last syllable of "Dijon", a nasal] near Tours, when we heard that Paris had fallen to the enemy siege without resistance. One true reason for my becoming a fighter pilot lay in my feeling that this Paris, this heart of my homeland, was being raped by a foreign force. Strange as it seems, though, I had literally never touched an airplane, nor even seen one up close during my, at that time, short life. Facing an important decision, I was undergoing a leap of faith, of courage, as it were. I was somewhat blinded by a sense of duty, by an engrained sentiment of honor, and I felt motivated by a law I'll call "humane justice." This must have come from my father.

This Camp Meucon had been a training camp for armored tank drivers of the First World War. These tanks were still in use, and we found a few of them around the place. During free time we would wriggle into these beasts and try to make them run. The controls were not at all complex: just an accelerator lever, operated by hand, and a left plus a right pedal, just like on the floor of an airplane. Airplane pedals control the tail, but these tank pedals were simply brakes: one left, one right. Press on one, and this was the way you were going to turn. We military recruits found this plenty amusing, since these little tanks closer resembled toys than weapons.

The regimen of military protocol, the respect for rank, the knowledge of weaponry and of course marching in formation, all now became the central focus of our lives. Foremost was the learning of combat discipline. Each man was issued one of those solid old Lebel rifles, heavy piece of equipment that it was. For marching we had to wear those heavy clodhoppers called *godillots* [pronounce goh-dee-YOH; this, long ago, was the family name of a purveyor of military shoes] with cleats in them! Can you believe it? These were not marching shoes at all. For everyday wear we were issued wooden sabots, shoes fabricated in Holland, and they gave us straw – yes, animal bedding – with which

CHAPTER 3   *War Breaks: 1940, I am Seventeen*   45

to keep our feet warm. Thinking back on it today, I can hardly believe it, so thank goodness I still have a photo or two.

My family and their safety worried me. Tino and all the rest of the people I knew in our nation's capital, what was going to become of them? How would Parisians react to all this? At this point I was only a few weeks away from being in England as Hitler was only a few weeks away from "touring" occupied Paris. These few weeks would prove crucial to the British as their time to beef up the enforcements.

My training near Tours was now behind me, noting how German advances caused the French military to shrink a matter of months for training into a matter of weeks. I was sent to the city of Vannes [pronounce VAHN] in Brittany, in the inland part of far western France. This was School #21, where* I would get to learn for real what an airplane was all about.

*   *   *

Our first assignments focused on maintenance, keeping the airplanes clean, and rolling them in and out of the hangar without damaging them. Janitorial work in the hangar was part of military service too, but for me, the undying optimist, it was just a joy to be up close and personal with these "birds." These models were called Stamps, Lucioles (a biplane) and Cri-cris [pronounce cree-cree].

I was proud of being able to identify and name different parts of a plane. There was the "broomstick", our *manche à balai*, which was in the middle of the interior. Moving this stick left and right, forward and back, you gave movement to your tail rudder and your ailerons. I studied hard and fast in hopes of piloting one of these birds.

Each morning we had classes on aerodynamics. They were teaching us how an airplane worked, the importance of its motor, of meteorology, of navigation. Every little bit was fascinating to me, especially when it came to identifying characteristics of

---

* Called "School #26" in error by other writers; I have handwritten orders showing "21" clearly.

enemy planes. We had to know their names, their capacities, the effectiveness of their weapons, how fast they could fly in pursuit and generally how to react when you encountered them in the sky. We were taught to speed up when we ran into enemy planes. They taught us to be careful to identify them properly, by silhouette at any distance, and to be sure not to fire upon our own guys by mistake.

Once the classroom part was over, we went on to practical training. One day we were all assembled outside. After a long silence, abruptly, the instructor said in a very serious tone, "Which one of you wants to take the stick?" The moment had come! Several hands shot up, and the instructor surveyed the group. His eyes stopped on me, and my heart skipped a beat. He motioned to me with his finger, saying, "Follow me," then, "By the way, are you sure you remember all the right moves?"

With a voice which was strong and sure, though my body was shaking like a leaf, I replied, "Oui, monsieur."

My time had come. I straightened my shoulders as I followed him, tremendously proud to be the chosen one among my jealous companions. We all walked over to a Luciole. Boy, was I excited! All tranquil, the instructor pulled a broom out of the fuselage, handing it to me, saying, "Show us how well you know this stick, how well you can sweep up the hangar. Maybe then I'll see if you are to be trusted with the real stick."

I was humiliated. The whole group left me there, laughing as they went. I concentrated on working quickly with the broom in order to put this unpleasant farce behind me. I felt like a Samaritan.

Well, well, to my happy surprise I got the instructor's promised reward. He let me choose any which plane I wanted for my training aircraft. Beside myself with joy, here I was inside the fuselage of my first plane, playing touchy-feely. I ran my hands lovingly up and down this infamous stick, making it move forward, backward and sideways. It was as if my dream was becoming reality. I was already seeing myself fighting enemy planes.

Two flight schools got merged into one. The merger was has-

CHAPTER 3   *War Breaks: 1940, I am Seventeen*   47

tened by the quick advance of the Germans. Also there was a shortage of supplies, equipment and instructors at School #21 of Vannes. Having finished classes and passed a test, off we went to School #23 near the city of Morlaix [pronounce mor-LAY]. Morlaix is in Brittany too, in far western France near Brest, where the English Channel joins the Atlantic. This all progressed with astonishing speed; pilots were in great demand.

Flight School: Morlaix, in Brittany

So, now it was our turn to get to fly for real. It was early June, 1940, and they were letting me solo! I was eighteen, not only according to my falsified documents, but my true eighteenth birthday had been Monday, June 3rd, 1940.

Keeping the flight logs for all of us student pilots was the job of one particular officer, and he was not a flight officer, since losing this key individual to a combat fatality would have meant a recordkeeping nightmare. This was different from the British system where each pilot or student pilot kept his own flight log, handing it in, on a weekly or monthly basis, to be compiled into a book for the whole Wing or Squadron. The British would redistribute the flight logs to the men, but I've been told that, for reasons of security, British pilots had to surrender these flight logs when they left the service. I still have mine, rubber stamp seal on every page. By the French system, one officer filled out many logbooks, then we pilots would be granted the right to take them with us at the end. Sadly my early flights do not appear in the two logbooks which I have, because records were lost as we escaped to England. Later I would make a *déclaration sur l'honneur*, a declaration on my honor, so I could show the hundred hours I had under my belt. Comprised mostly of take-offs and landings, a whole day of training often showed as just 30 minutes, so a hundred hours were pretty important.

At the beginning, of course, I was taught using dual controls whereby the instructor helped me take off, also land without making too many hops and skips. You had to sort of touch down the way a feather duster slides on a table, without any bounce. The idea of dual controls was to give the student a feeling of control yet maintain safety in the event the student got nervous or anxious. The role of the instructor was primarily to transmit confidence into his students, letting the student perform the indicated maneuvers, all the while guiding the student verbally. This would inevitably lead to a point where the instructor no longer needed to touch the controls, where simply a verbal instruction would suffice. Instructors used a great deal of psychology, knowing we were both apprehensive and genuinely capable of messing up. So, like a big brother, the instructor would guide a student, encourage him, direct him, constantly reassure him as progress was made toward getting him to overcome his fears.

I will forever remember myself at age eighteen and my first solo! It was a very clear morning. My instructor and I had just completed three takeoffs and landings. Before the fourth time up, my instructor hopped out, saying, "Drabier, hold the controls 'til I get back. There's a pressing matter I must take care of." The motor was turning at a low rpm. I saw the instructor distance himself, his back turned, so he could empty his bladder.

Alone for the first time in this little plane, boy, I was proud. I squeezed on those handles as if I'd never let loose, verifying that the gauge was reading proper idle speed. This motor really purred at idle. My noble instructor came back, a wide smile on his face, then he looked me right in the eye and said, "Hey, you're coming along pretty good. Go on, take off! And bring me back an airplane with a perfect landing."

I thought my heart was going to jump right out of my chest! Wide-eyed, I stared fixedly straight ahead, and as if guided by an unknown force my hand pushed the handle all the way down. I lifted off. Up at about six hundred feet, a bigger picture of reality presented itself in my mind: I foresaw myself in dogfights with the enemy.

I finished up my flight just fine, touching down like an ace. I had earned my student-pilot "wing." This first insignia had only one wing and the two winged version, which was otherwise the

CHAPTER 3 *War Breaks: 1940, I am Seventeen*

same, came later. You were a student pilot, or *élève-pilote*, only once, but in the future you could indeed become, for a brief time as you familiarized yourself with a new plane, a pilot student, or *pilote élève*, again and again. We French used the English term "cockpit drill" to describe what we had to do as pilot students, familiarizing ourselves with new instruments.

*   *   *

Every single morning I was out there on the field to learn more about this Luciole, this silvery beauty of a biplane with two open-air cockpits. The Luciole had been one of the most popular privately owned airplanes in aero-clubs of the 1930s, but remember the whole idea of airborne movement was new to me. I performed all my in-flight exercises, especially practicing recovering from a planned shutdown where we would cut the motor. This required us to glide as we rapidly searched out a spot on the ground to touch down.

We made figure-eight (8) descents which, unlike an approach in a straight line, distracted you from controlling your altitude. The final hundred and fifty vertical feet of descent as you came in for a landing were crucial. We also had precision landings starting from varying altitudes. We had to slow the motor down and land within limits established by red panels on the ground. We had to put the plane right in the middle. Not to the right, not to the left, but right in the middle, and Lucioles did not have brakes!

The long awaited day came for us to learn to fly in tight formation, first by twos, then threes. When finally well enough trained and more confident, we'd learn to fly as a regular fighter squadron, that is, six forming a cross. Our top instructor had us get in order on the ground, he himself up front, ready for takeoff. Then the sky turned dark and the wind started to whip, just when the motors were properly warmed up. This is a very important precaution against fuel's not burning properly, since misfires can delay individual takeoffs and most especially make it dangerous to fly in tight formation. After rapid decisionmaking, the mission got called off for inclement weather.

We all headed for the tent which served as a pilot briefing room, since it had a radio permanently situated there for news and weather. We listened to it as we took off our gear and transmitted flight log information to the record-keeper. The news was bad: the Germans were already at the city of Rennes [pronounce ren; two hundred miles past Paris, that is west of Paris, also in the Brittany region where we were] and they were coming farther west toward Saint-Malo and Saint-Brieuc. We were sure we'd never make it south to the Atlantic port city of Lorient as planned.

The New Government

On Friday June 14th, 1940, Paris was occupied. That same Sunday, June 16th, Paul Reynaud resigned as Prime Minister. French President Lebrun entrusted the forming of the new government to Marshal (an honorary military title) Philippe Pétain, born in 1856 so he was age 84. Pétain* "formed" the Vichy Government. Later on, Marshal Pétain would rendezvous with Adolf Hitler at the infamous October 24th, 1940, "Interview of Montoire-sur-le-Loir" (just north of the city of Tours, central France, Tours being on La Loire river). It would be at that time when Hitler would give him the order to advance and to fire upon sailors, aviators… French soldiers! Frenchman against Frenchman? The Free French Forces, of which we were to become a part, got accused of being mercenaries, of being traitors. "All those who resist will be taken prisoner and executed."

THE CALL TO ARMS OF
GENERAL DE GAULLE: JUNE 18TH, 1940

TO ALL FRENCH LISTENERS
France has lost the battle,
but France has not lost the war!
Some governing persons found themselves able to capitulate,

Pétain: 1945 condemned to death at age 89, sentence commuted, died 1951 in exile

CHAPTER 3   War Breaks: 1940, I am Seventeen

giving in to panic,
foregoing honor, delivering the Country into servitude.
But all is not lost.
Nothing is lost, because this war is a world war.
In our universe which loves freedom, some immense forces have not yet come to bear.
One day, these forces will crush the enemy.
France must, upon that day, be present at the victory.
She will then re-establish her liberty and her grandeur.
This is my goal, my one and only goal!
This is why I call upon all French persons, wherever they may be,
to unite with me in action, in sacrifice and in hope.
Our Motherland is in danger of being killed.
Let us all fight to save her! VIVE LA FRANCE !

On June 18th, 1940, a Tuesday just two days after Reynaud had resigned, we followed our orders* to bug out: the Beginners' Pilot Training School #23 was to leave Morlaix. It was seven o'clock in the morning. We got the direct order of Lieutenant Pinot via Second Lieutenant Berthier to go to Quimper, a river port of Brittany, just south of where we were, some 340 miles west of Paris. Off we went in trucks. Not planes, but covered troop transport trucks.

Advancing German Forces: We get Overrun

We had to leave a number of Luciole airplanes behind. We destroyed them so the Germans wouldn't make use of them, and it was heartbreaking for me to see those precious little planes, skin made of silver-colored fabric, reduced to scrap.

It was at the stroke of noon on that Tuesday, June 18th, 1940, when we arrived at Quimper in the region of Brittany. Each of us

---

* Translator's note: Jacques originally wrote up this departure to be 24 or 48 hours later. Our research renders "after midnight of 18 June, that is extremely early the 19th, a Wednesday" very, very credible. What Jacques calls "war-important speed" explains his perspective and perception. A sort of time warp was forced on these young men; Jacques used the words "minds spinning like I don't know what." Jacques was seeing the number of preparatory movements they went through as too much for "same day" escape from France; 18 June was the date of General de Gaulle's appeal via British Broadcast Corporation radio.

had carried along one little suitcase, some guys just a single little sack in one hand, and before Lieutenant Pinot would even let us stow the little we had, he insisted on inspecting the troops. He seemed anxious, wanting to verify that the whole group had really gotten there, and he was responsible for more than just our school. Lieutenant Pinot, age 49 at the time, had been the mechanic for Georges Guynemer [pronounce guee-nuh-MEHR], the World War I ace with over fifty kills. A few Lucioles had been flown this little distance, under a hundred and fifty miles, by the instructors. My memory says they were Georges Le Dilasser, Fernand Poulain, Robert Nioloux, Jean Lecouté, plus Roger Le Poulennec, and my memory is clear that they transported some materials from our abandoned school. Somehow we wound up taking those archaic Lewis machineguns that we used to use for practice without firing them. Not having the right ammo, these got tossed overboard, in case some scuba diver of a reader picks up on this.

We were unable to contact the Third Division, but in a freak occurrence Second Lieutenant Berthier found himself on the horn with some Germans. A quick decision was called for. A reliable source was telling us that the southeasterly route, via Nantes on the Loire River in order to wind up south of the Loire, was out of the question. No arguing it: this route was too dangerous.

Via telephone, Lieutenant Pinot reached the French authorities at the city of Brest, in the opposite direction, that is to say on the tip of Brittany jutting out into the Atlantic. His query to them was if a sea route might work for evacuating his schoolboys, his precious* students of Flight School number 23 of Morlaix. Could they get us to Morocco, south of Spain, by boat?

The Navy was unable to help. The Prefect, or Mayor, of the city of Quimper suggested, even insisted, that everyone stay put. He was saying we should twiddle our thumbs, as he offered no escape whatsoever. Luckily Lieutenant Pinot was not at all in

---

* Affectionate terms like this are widely acknowledged in other readings. Confer *Bonsoir Nadette,* 2004, a French publication, page 5, fourth paragraph, "...these 'little guys' [*petits gars*], I'd travel to the ends of the Earth for them."

CHAPTER 3 War Breaks: 1940, I am Seventeen

agreement, and he discussed things briefly with Second Lieutenant Berthier. The two of them were in accord that we had to act fast or be in the clutches of the enemy within hours.

Berthier took the required course of action. Off by car he went to the city of Brest to see if he could find a boat, at any price, which could take him and his student pilots, well, somewhere! What awaited us in France was like a flood of biblical proportions. Along the way he bumped into some naval officers who suggested he try the port town of Douarnenez. One of the naval officers went with Berthier, and by the best of luck they found a Monsieur François Lelguen, operator of a fishing boat. The diary of Flight Sergeant Hauchemaille states we might have taken a ship by force if required to do so.

Our group, then, headed for Douarnenez, a fishing village on an inwardly curved stretch of coast, only twenty miles from Quimper where we were. Monsieur Lelguen and Second Lieutenant Berthier reached some kind of agreement to evacuate School #23 aboard the *Trébouliste* [pronounce tray-bool-EEST], named for the smaller fishing village called Tréboul, and it was a good solution to our problem. The *Trébouliste* was a seventy-foot-long Dundee style (after the Scottish port named Dundee) fishing vessel. It was a two mast sailboat with a sixty horsepower auxiliary motor which chugged along at three miles per hour. Under normal circumstances, it would have been harvesting fish off the coast of the region called Mauritania on the Atlantic coast of Africa just south of Morocco.

Our Escape: 18 JUNE 1940

Monsieur Lelguen had just brought the *Trébouliste* back in from a "high risk" fishing venture: her sister ship, the *Julien DZ3252*, had been sunk by a German submarine only a month earlier off the coast of Spain. Even though her crew had successfully gotten away from the wreck and had returned to Douarnenez, local spirits were impacted by the event. Lelguen had just barely stepped ashore when he met up with Berthier and Duprat, our emissaries. Negotiations must have gone quickly in this state of urgency, but we, the students of School #23, were orderly as we proceeded toward Douarnenez at 9:30pm that Tuesday, June 18, 1940. A quiet, subdued state prevailed, a natural result of not knowing, at our young age, if death was around the corner.

We got to the little section of the waterfront called *Le Port du Rosmeur* [pronounce luh por dew rohz-MEUR] about 10:15pm. The tide was out and the *Trébouliste* was unable to make it to the dock. In the midst of a black night, the embarkation began about 11:15pm. By 1:30am on Wednesday, June 19th, 1940, we were underway. The crew had been reduced from its normal size to just five, yet the sails got hoisted and off we went, the bow due north.

The boat passed Newlyn, England on June 20th, Thursday, at noon, then proceeded to Falmouth where she got in at 10pm. Right away, we were warmly welcomed by the British.

We who escaped via the *Trébouliste* were the students of School #23, its officers, plus some older pilots like Jules Joire, plus some local guys. Over half died war heroes. A good portion of them, I included, became the core of the *Forces Aériennes Françaises Libres* (hereafter "F.A.F.L.") which was the Free French Air Force, and the *Forces Navales Françaises Libres* which was the Free French Navy.

Writing about those guys onboard brings me sadness even six and a half decades later. They sacrificed their lives for the motherland, denying what was truthfully a legitimate government called "Vichy", wanting France to be free. I recognize their faces in photographs, but both time and age have a way of taking away memory for names. There were over fifty of us, and these are guys I used to go out for a drink with, or practice sports with, and with whom I certainly exchanged confidences. Maurice Vergès, F.A.F.L.#30443, was my best friend, a true compatriot, almost a brother. We evaded the Nazis there on the *Trébouliste* and continued on the same course together until 1943 in Syria, a bifurcation in our paths. I would go off to Morocco to fly fighter aircraft

CHAPTER 3 War Breaks: 1940, I am Seventeen

whereas he went the route of flying bombers. Still during the war, we met up later in England where he was flying a bomber, the B-26 which was named The Marauder. Maurice flew plenty of missions, and just like me he came out of the war intact.

Later on, in 1946, I would choose not to pursue a military career. Three months of Occupation service in Germany, in the French zone near the city of Trier on the Moselle River, were enough for me, so I sought my discharge papers. Maurice chose commercial aviation as a career. I had the great pleasure of seeing him in Paris, just once, at the end of 1945, after the war. Soon enough I would be off to Canada in 1953 and emigrated to the U.S.A. in 1959.

I had another really good buddy, Gilbert Vaillant, #30051 F.A.F.L., and he was attached to a very active squadron numbered 340 and called "*Île de France*" [pronounce eel duh FRAHNSS]. He met his death in a midair collision in 1943. My buddy Roger Le Poulennec, #30502 F.A.F.L., died in an accident during takeoff in 1942; he was with the 66th Squadron. Our instructor died for France too: Flight Sergeant Marc Hauchemaille, F.A.F.L. number 30105, became a Second Lieutenant with the 340th Squadron and was shot down by a German fighter and reported missing 27 April, 1942. Georges Le Dilasser, F.A.F.L. #30130, was killed in flight in an accident along his route of Cairo-Beirut in May of 1942. There were many more in those fighter groups named for Alsace, for Lorraine and for other regions.

Our "*Bouboule*" [pronounce boo-BOOL], a French nickname for a chubby guy, was the infamous Édouard Pinot, F.A.F.L. #30171, and Commander of Morlaix Flight School #23. He was onboard the *Trébouliste* and is easily identifiable in the photos [web search: *Trebouliste* 1940]. A true hero, he too finished the war intact, and I remember Pinot's being as down-to-earth as an officer ever should be. He died in 1984, age 93 or 94, in I know not what condition.

Records show* that of fifty to eighty students onboard the *Trébouliste*, over thirty died for France between 1940 and 1945. Two or three of the eleven non-commissioned officers died for France by 1945. Both Berthier and Pinot survived. Some statisticians give the nationwide pilots' death rate at over sixty percent, which would be to say only three or four out of ten survive the war. Jean Lecouté, three years older than me, F.A.F.L. #30118, who finished the war with honors, died of leukemia in 1990. As of 2007, René Moine, born July 31st, 1920, F.A.F.L. #30289, and I, Jacques Drabier, born June 3rd, 1922, F.A.F.L. #30221 are, I think, the only surviving adventurers of the *Trébouliste* odyssey. It was such a Point of Karma in the mysterious swerves and turns of my life, I begin the next chapter with a more thorough account of this trip across the English Channel, and by telling it we'll meet "*Bouboule*" and read a fabulous quote from his mouth to my ears.

---

* Appendix to *Bonsoir Nadette,* Philippe Chéron, 2004.

CHAPTER 3   *War Breaks: 1940, I am Seventeen*

Morlaix Flight School, 1940.
A group at the beach near Dinard.
See "me" upper right.

On the deck of the *Trébouliste*,
1940, escaping to England

War Pilot Memoirs: A Mirror on 1939

CHAPTER 4

Quote: *"Do We just Yield, into Custom-made Nooses?"*

Our Escape aboard a Lobster Boat

It was decided that there be enough food and water for twice the expected time at sea, so each man was to bring only the minimum of personal belongings. Many brought their diaries. Flight Sergeant Hauchemaille was killed at war, yet his diary would become a book. Lieutenant Pinot ("Bouboule") requisitioned the food supplies, which got there fast.

The order was given that supper be a quick one. At twenty-one thirty, that is 9:30 on Tuesday evening 18 JUNE 1940, with remarkable calm, we formed a convoy column. From Quimper we made the twenty mile trek to the port town of Douarnenez, without headlights by virtue of security. The tide was low. I vividly recall the little boats we used to get out to the *Trébouliste*, which for lack of water could not make it to the dock. It was almost midnight. Weapons, namely Gras [pronounce grah] brand rifles and those Lewis machineguns from the School, ammunition and food supplies went on first, then bags, then us.

Second Lieutenant Berthier, at the order of Lieutenant Pinot, let it be known that England was where this boat would land, and that each man was free to stay or go. Lieutenant Pinot used* this simple but heartfelt language:

My Guys! (He liked to use this expression *Mes petits*

---

* Over 65 years of time make it impossible to recall these words without help, so my thanks go to Ms. L'Herbier Montagnon for *Cap sans retour*, 1948.

gars when he got emotional.) They're asking us to lay down our arms and wait for the Krauts, just to hand ourselves over to them **as if we had custom tailored nooses around our necks.** Do you guys think we French can do that? The Krauts are three hours away. Several of your superiors, that is, several of your instructors and I, have decided to leave. I have to tell you the trip will involve some risk, maybe being bombed, maybe underwater mines or submarines, maybe being boarded en route for inspection. Danger will not be lacking. In so many words, we may die out there. But in my opinion this risk is far better than falling into the hands of the Krauts.

Anyway, that's what I have to say.

Our Flight School #23 saw at least sixty-four of its own climb aboard: two officers, eleven* non-comms. and fifty-one students. Modern-day research gives these numbers, but I firmly believe there were more of us. Not even the protection of souls was lacking: the Chaplain, Father Godard, was one of the eleven. With the ship's captain and some locals accounting for twenty or thirty more, it was crowded on that boat no longer than a tractor-trailer truck, yet our mascot dog Pilou [pronounce pee-LOO] went also.

Lieutenant Pinot and Second Lieutenant Berthier were the last two onboard the *Trébouliste*. The English port city Newlyn was told to us as the compass heading to steer for. Anchors aweigh was Wednesday, June 19th, at 1:30 in the morning. We student pilots lent a hand, and the power came from the wind in her sails so the ship could proceed as silently as possible. The townsfolk of Douarnenez came out in force, yet they were quiet, watching these boys go off into the night.

Once out at sea, far off there appeared the glimmering of fire destroying the French arsenal at Brest. It must have been a bright fire; we would have come within thirty miles at the closest. Adieu to the land of France; a vibrant rendition of the national anthem, "La Marseillaise", did strike up. Overcome with patriotic emotion, many of us had tears trickling down our cheeks.

---

* In French, these non-commissioned ranks were *sergent* + *sergent-chef*; see page LXIII, *Bonsoir Nadette*, 2004.

The Grand Adventure Begins

There were two machineguns which were functional, to a degree. These were set up, one on the starboard side and one on the port side, thinking that sunrise might bring an aircraft attack. We certainly hoped it wouldn't be from a submarine.

The sea was rough, and the *Trébouliste* pitched and rolled. Some Douarnenez locals onboard were seamen, but almost all of us young non-seafarers got sick. We were sad enough to be taken away from our families, from our lovers, from our country, and frankly we were wiped out. The *Trébouliste* rolled side to side, pitched forward and aft. Seasickness is no easy matter, but neither is homesickness. Then again, at least seasickness kept our minds off the enemy.

Onboard there was quite a stir when airplanes, which weren't always identifiable, flew over from time to time. A little tuna or lobster boat must have seemed too small to be of interest to enemy pilots. As to Allied planes, I specifically recall a Hurricane which had loudspeakers underneath. We were about to miss Newlyn, near Penzance, the last major port on the Channel before Land's End which is the extreme southwest tip of England. The Hurricane was a one-seater just like most fighters, and that pilot tipped his wings to get our attention, then he corrected our course. We encountered several warships, and luckily all were French or British.

Another time two Messerschmitts flew over so low they almost clipped the masts, so low that the swastikas in their paint jobs were distinctly visible. As they prepared to fly back around, since they had not fired on us the first time over, all the officers were hollering, "Play dead. Don't move!" The two planes flew back around, but again they didn't fire. Oof! What happened? Maybe our assembly of wayfarers on a little boat didn't seem important enough to bother with.

It was under a clear blue sky that we first saw the coast of Britain, having endured about thirty-six hours in the waters of the English Channel. Second Lieutenant Berthier, whose knowledge of the English language would be invaluable to us, went ashore about 12 noon on Thursday, June 20th, 1940, to seek instructions on where to go. He got back at 15 hundred hours, mid-afternoon, saying that Falmouth would be the port of entry. Remember that the *Trébouliste* was a two-mast sailing vessel under eighty feet long with a diesel motor for auxiliary power only. Our dear Captain Lelguen said Falmouth, only twenty miles away by land but a full fifty miles away by sea, would take forever with those contrary winds. A British steamer, *Lady Estelle*, towed us to Falmouth where we arrived late the same night.

We hopped aboard a barge of the British Navy which pulled up alongside, and we transferred all the gear too. Disembarkation at the dock took place right away at thirty minutes after midnight. Finally, officers and men alike, fatigued to the limit, stretched out on the dock and went to sleep under the stars. We were nothing more than driftwood at this point. Having used a steel rail for a pillow, one expatriated fellow woke up with a crick in his neck, yet happy to be alive.

The British did all they could to make us Frenchmen comfortable. First English meal? Corned beef, potatoes and tea. It was not very good. The British allies, though, were so helpful that their kindness was the essence of a second nature. If an Englander gave you a cigarette, he'd feel guilty if he didn't light it for you.

ENGLAND: Trentham

The next day was June 22nd, 1940, and 2pm saw the whole group onboard a train bound for Trentham Park. The arrival there was around midnight that Saturday night. Uncomfortably, we finished out this night onboard the train. Sunday, June 23rd, seven days after Pétain and the Vichyists had come into power, oh-six-hundred (6am), we of Flight School #23 reported to the camp. They called all of us Frenchmen together, which is to say there

CHAPTER 4 *Quote: "Do We just Yield...?"*

were others there who had come by other means than the *Trébouliste*.

It was raining cats and dogs, but the tents had to be set up. These were those big eleven-man tents. There was a meal, if you can call it that: a huge can of tuna to share, little tidbits of a strange bread, plus a can of jelly. If my mother had witnessed this meal, she'd never have gotten over it, and if my Assam had witnessed it she'd have yanked me out of there. Some of the tents got put up crooked, so a few of us had rainwater as if channeled in by gargoyles.

What in the world were the Vichyists back in France saying? That we were rebels? Now that was the last straw. We wanted to go about preparing to fight a wicked enemy, and they were insulting us? In my heart, I knew that we were right and that history would prove it.

*   *   *

Good fortune, a favorable turn of Destiny, came our way on June 27th, 1940, the Thursday in the same week of that Sunday we had pitched the wet tents. School number twenty-three traveled by train to a Royal Air Force installation near Saint Athan, twenty miles from Cardiff on the coast of Wales and just over a hundred miles due west of London. We arrived in the evening and were greeted in the warmest way. Oh, my God, these were evermore creature comforts: beds, hot and cold running water, showers, swimming pool, movie projector. Nothing was lacking.

What a lucky stroke. To boot, we got paid five shillings, only a few hours' worth of wages to a manual laborer in those days, but a godsend to us. We would have loved to spend it on a decent glass of wine, because... that damned tea, you know! But it would buy plenty of glasses of whisky, so life was ok.

It was a nuisance that these British didn't speak what we did. I set out to overcome this, as I garnered all my courage to go about learning English.

Camberley
Bombing of London, and I First Meet my future Wife

In the big picture of History, what the Allies did at Camberley seems rather unique. The reader should bear in mind that my perspective was a "bottom up" view through the eyes of an 18-year-old, for what it may be worth. We seemed to be all kinds of guys coming in from every direction. Some showed up looking like hobos, some well dressed. All of us had our pedigrees investigated, though, and the concept of "patriotic school" as opposed to "concentration camp" would be a news reporter's way of making it sound above board. We of School #23 owed our relatively quick processing through Camberley to Lieutenant "Bouboule" Pinot and his good politicking. I think it was a cousin to Churchill who was his political connection, and Pinot had invoked this connection upon our landing at Falmouth. We of School #23 were not immune to German spies, however, because one of the *Trébouliste* passengers had been executed by firing squad back at Falmouth; I had personally witnessed this.

Camberley, just thirty miles southwest of central London, also focused us on becoming military. We learned about ranks, we were issued uniforms, and we marched. We had classes on technical terms of the English language, yet many of us discovered the "pillow method" for learning a language. That is to say we dated the English girls.

During my time near the city of Camberley I was often allowed off-base on weekend leave. London was just a half hour away: local "omnibus" trains, which stopped at every station, circulated in the suburbs, or we were permitted to use a truck sometimes.

German planes were dropping bombs every night that the weather permitted. Radar was not yet widely used and German pilots didn't like venturing into the pea soup. The British had lived with this fog all their lives, and they were happy at how it hindered the Reich. The British had dotted the skies with dirigibles at varying altitudes, and these were undetectable to Ger-

CHAPTER 4 *Quote: "Do We just Yield...?"*

man airplanes. Back then, planes navigated by simple compasses and radiolocators triangulated to keep them on course. When cloudbanks were not too thick, the Germans bombed London blindly, without even seeing the ground. The devastation was monstrous. They'd get a dose of English "spit fire" on the way back, though, since the cloudbanks typically thinned out at the coastline.

On leave in London, you became numb to the sound of exploding bombs. You just got so used to it. On the other hand, the bombs would cause your skin to crawl, not knowing where they were going to fall. If you felt the vibration of a bomb a little too close, you'd follow the Londoners into their bomb shelters.

The Krauts had invented a new type of large diameter bomb weighing about a ton. They dropped it dangling under a parachute, so it had the look of a big kettle swinging over a fire. This "kettle" did a lot of damage, and we French said "*la marmite*" to refer to it. This was well before the time of V-1 missiles.

*   *   *

One particular night I was headed for Olympia Hall. The night was serene with a gorgeous moon. To myself I was thinking how those Heinkel one-eleven bombers and those Dorniers must love a night like this for precision bombing.

At Picadilly Circus, where Olympia Hall was located, it was a lovely evening. This hall was renowned as the nicest one around, and I loved to dance. The interior was spectacular with its dance floor built to accommodate five hundred couples. The bandstand, which was lighted, was a turnstile. They changed bands every hour, and the music was the best of Glenn Miller, Benny Goodman or Harry James with his infamous jazz band. When our fighter pilots nowadays have their reunions, understandably this is the music we still like to hear.

In Olympia Hall, tables were assigned to branches of the military, both French and English, so, shall we say, aviation had its privileges. One thing that struck me as strange was the way all those pretty girls were standing there along the wall, since the reserved tables were for soldiers. The only difficulty for us guys was a plethora of choice when it came to dance partners. A lady would only sit at one of the tables when invited. My best friend Maurice Vergès and I had each picked out a girl. Off went Maurice with a little brunette since Maurice himself was a little squirt, and I chose a ravishing blonde named Vera. She was an excellent dancer, which led us to spend the entire evening on the dance floor, experiencing that inebriating joy which people in all times and places have known.

Alas, all good things must come to an end, and the time came to go back to camp. Vera and I didn't fail to set a rendezvous for a week later at Trafalgar Square. There was a large metro-rail station there, so it made a good meeting place. She would be coming in by train from the city of Horsham in Sussex County where her parents lived, and I would be coming by truck. Horsham is south of London and it's about twenty miles before you get to the coast. We agreed on the place and time, and I was even then planning to invite her for a nice meal at the Red Lyon, a well-reputed restaurant, and then we'd go dancing.

We parted. Looking forward to seeing her again brought me that heart-flutter which young men, and I suppose young ladies, enjoy as a grace of youth. Let's just say she was my flavor. We said our goodbyes and I headed over to the trucks which faithfully awaited us soldiers. We needed to hurry because those sirens with their sinister tone were already squealing out an air raid warning, rupturing the silence of the night. Far off you could hear German planes and the debut of exploding bombs on the ground. Once I heard a female passerby say, "The Jerries are busy again, thanks to the moon." This became a typical British expression, and it was based on truth.

My military friends all came running up at once. Scurrying, everybody was saying goodbye to his girlfriend. The danger of shrapnel was on the way, so the truck pulled out in a hurry. Driving away, we looked back to see London on fire. Such a pretty city, it has always seemed a particular shame to me.

My Second Leave

When the week was up, I obtained leave once again to go to London. I thought that this leave was going to be very special. Unknown to me, it was going to be one of the most dramatic and frightening experiences of my life.

We pulled into Trafalgar Square in our trucks, and the night was pitch black. Since air raids were frequent, it was preferable not to use headlights and such. What you could see around you in the streets were scintillating little points of light like fireflies. Car headlights were camouflaged, so just passersby could see them, and so drivers could see somewhat where they were going.

This particular night the fog seemed thicker than usual. I recall how worried I was about stepping into a pothole, since visibility was down to about five feet. I found my way to the North exit of Trafalgar Station, our rendezvous spot, where I expected to find my little blonde, Vera, since I knew I was right on time. There was quite a crowd, but Vera had not arrived, so maybe I was early? Abruptly, the sirens started going off. Just as quickly, everybody scurried for cover. This enormous station itself was good cover. You would simply descend the steps to the bottom where you'd find corridors equipped with furniture and separate rooms set up as air raid shelters. I continued looking for Vera, and I was getting a bit anxious. A non-military monitor with a white insignia on his sleeve, indicating he was one who helped direct people to shelter, politely said, "Sir, you must get below." We were already hearing bombs blowing up. I saw other military men across the street going down into a different bunker, so I decided to go follow them. I galloped across that street, and just as those soldiers and I got to the safety of that refuge, one enormous explosion made itself felt and heard. The whole world was shaking, it seemed. From our side of the street you could see dust and debris flying everywhere. Some of the debris struck hard enough to demolish the door on our side. We waited patiently for the sirens to stop, being the signal, generally, that people could safely come out of their lair.

Oh my God, such carnage! What a display! Half of Trafalgar Square had been transformed into crumbling stone, and smoke and dust filled the atmosphere. Right away the noble firemen went to work, placing barricades across the entranceways, or rather what used to be entranceways. What was left now were big, deep holes in the ground. Later we learned that a "kettle" bomb under parachute had fallen at the main entrance. The "kettle" had descended via the moving escalator which, for unknown reasons, had not ceased functioning as it was supposed to. Thus the "kettle" had found its way to the bottom of the installation before exploding, killing about a hundred and fifty men, women and children.

Not a single survivor came out of that shelter. It would be necessary simply to wall up the entrance, and with tons of powdered lime poured into the hole the entire thing would be covered over. Neither time nor means to bring out the bodies. You always had to think of the next air raid coming, which would put everybody in danger. My hair stood on end, because this was the very spot where Vera and I had planned to meet!

It would have been very logical for me to go down into that first shelter. Why had I decided to cross the street and seek refuge with the other soldiers? I was supposed to meet Vera here. Where in the world was she? Was she down there amongst those poor souls? I could not let myself believe it. With anxiety pinching at my heart, I ducked into a phone booth which miraculously was functional. I dialed the number she'd given me. I was able to talk to her parents who told me Vera had already phoned to say that the electric train she was on had stopped operating, just as it should, when the air raid had begun. She was, therefore, two miles away from the appointed rendezvous spot. I could breathe now. What fate. A lucky twist was playing its strange role on me. My pretty blonde was safe and sound, but if the train had failed to stop… she'd have rolled into Trafalgar where I was, before I decided to cross the street!

All these emotional trials somewhat behind us, I got invited by Vera's parents, Mr. and Mrs. Wells of the city of Horsham, to come visit. They absolutely wanted to meet me, to get to know this aviator for Free France.

*   *   *

The quaint suburbs in which Horsham lay were absolutely charming, and I noticed it most acutely on my first visit. A very calm place, all the houses resembled each other, standing there in timeless peace one next to another. I bumped into the mailman, whom I asked for directions to the Wells' house. "Oh, yes," he retorted, "the chimneysweep! Just go down that way, next to the big tree, just a hundred yards from where you're standing." Later I came to know that Vera's father, a retiree, did part time work as a chimneysweep, supplementing his pension.

I found the right house. I rang. A man with a bit of age on him, with white hair, opened the door for me. Seeing my uniform, he said, "Oh, you must be the French pilot that Lottie talks about. Please, please, come in." I noticed a lady with a wide smile on her face standing behind him.

I approached her and presented some flowers and the traditional box of chocolates, and she said, "By George, what a jolly box. All for me?"

A very delicious aroma was coming from the kitchen. Without any ado, Mrs. Wells led me into the kitchen, which was surely the most frequented room in this house. She had me sit, and very graciously she offered me a cup of tea, and from a shelf she got down some very typical English cookies. Mr. Albert Wells looked me straight in the face and said, "Well, you're the young man Lottie's been talking to me about. Didn't the two of you win a dance trophy your last time at Olympia Hall?" He was reaching over to shake my hand when I noticed how his hands were very black. He held back, perhaps noticing a little hesitation on my part. He pulled a shilling coin or two out of his pocket as he said, "I'm sorry, but I just got back from sweeping chimneys. Even when you wash your hands for all you're worth, some of the black remains, embedded in your skin. But the money is clean!" He wanted to make a point. The soot on his hands represented just how he'd earned this honest money. In that era, chimneysweeps were in high demand. Most people burned wood in the furnace for heating the house. An aroma of unburned pinewood permeated the air in these regions, and it was very special.

Lottie was a nickname used in the family for Vera. She arrived, with her sister Connie, who was a bit taller. Connie was married to Darcy Johnson who was a farmer and who also rented farm equipment to other nearby farmers. Connie took care of the barnyard, which included raising those infamous Sussex County chickens, renowned for their special eggs owing to the feed they got. I kissed Connie on the cheek after my cordial but shy greeting, and with an impish grin, a bold and wide grin, she said, "Well, well, Mister Pilot, we like my sister, do we?"

I blushed a little as I tried to sketch out a reply in my mind to this unexpected question. "Hmm. I thought it was my little secret," was all I could muster. We struck up a conversation by which I learned that Connie already had a little boy Trevor and a daughter Pauline.

Another thing I learned from Connie was how the British government, when it had declared war on Germany in 1939, had made a universal appeal to the populace. Anyone who could not serve in the military should be actively engaged in the manufacture of such things as uniforms, weaponry, or in specialized sectors like pharmaceuticals or nursing.

Connie said the government also made exception as to military service for those who were tilling the soil; England would feed her troops. I found out that Vera helped on the farm sometimes. In contrast to this, Vera had tried pharmacy work but had found that poking pills into boxes or stirring up liquids all day long was not her strong suit. Vera also didn't want to join the military, so she needed to make some kind of career decision. After reflecting, I politely recommended to her that she try nurs-

CHAPTER 4 *Quote: "Do We just Yield...?"*

ing which was in huge demand. She said she thought this sounded pretty good, but I suspect that in part she was placating me. She signed up right away for a program of study lasting three years.

We decided to get engaged, and it was met with resounding approval by her family, so I was accepted as one of their own. Sister Connie took charge of organizing the festivities. I knew the family was not financially well endowed, so I suggested, without offending anyone, that I take on the expense of the engagement party; I pulled this off pretty well. A good number of their friends were to be invited, all quite curious to meet this French pilot. The ambiance was very quaintly English, but so was the food.

Prior to such grand festivities as these, it was necessary to have a go at the village pub, to sample some fine beer. My preference was for dark beer, and as to my future father-in-law, by God, he was one who could drain four or five pints of the stuff without batting an eye! I, on the other hand, once into my second glass typically found myself at my limit. Mr. Wells took the grandest pleasure at trying to drink me under the table, all for the bolstering of his own pride, yet he was goodhearted about it. Many a time I would plot to myself how to get even someday and put him under the table.

It would be much later, 1945, when I'd get revenge. This would be my wedding when I'd be in charge of selecting the beverages: no beer, but an assortment of fine wines to reflect the French spirit. Needless to say that occasion saw my father-in-law on the floor, and I would savor the event, but without malice. Mr. Wells was a fine man and to my misfortune I never got to know him well enough, since just after this 1945 wedding I'd have to go back for military service. He died in 1946 at age seventy-seven without seeing our paths cross again. This made me sad, since we really did get along well. I believe he was appreciative of the fact I was fighting for his country as well as mine.

My Grand Adventures in Britain's Restaurants

We of the Army Air Corps had just been issued khaki uniforms. The boat-shaped hat, a light blue, had a metal Royal Air Force eagle pinned to it on the left side. To distinguish us from others wearing the same uniform, the word "French" (in English) was embroidered in a white patch that belonged at the top of the left sleeve. We ourselves had to stitch this white patch on carefully, since there were many nationalities, specifically Belgian, Canadian and Polish.

One particular evening we French were out in a group of five or six, and we'd decided we deserved a nice meal at that fine restaurant The Red Lyon. The plan was to regale ourselves with a good steak and some chips, which was what the British called their French fries. We got seated, and as usual the restaurant was filled to capacity, including plenty of uniforms, since soldiers knew the best places to eat. The waiters had no idea that we weren't British, because there we sat in those R.A.F. uniforms. The waiter came over to our table to take the order. We spoke very little English, and even this little bit was all about mechanical gizmos and certainly not culinary terms. The waiter, with a typical benign smirk of a smile, in an English jargon he thought was being addressed to RAFs, said, "What'll it be?"

My buddies looked at me, giving me the go-ahead to place the order, so I set myself to it with a less than assured air about me. With my index finger I counted around the table, in English, "One, two, three, four, five, six steaks."

The waiter replied, "How would you like your steaks?"

In a hurry, I set myself to conjuring up the word for "*saignant*" in English. The literal translation, "bloody", was what I gave to the waiter, not knowing the more proper word "rare." The British swearwords of choice in this era were "bloody" followed by "f_ _ _ing", and they slapped these words into darned near every sentence. Maintaining his benign smile, our waiter stared at me, thinking I was being a smart aleck, and came back with, "Ok, with some bloody f_ _ _ing chips, right?"

CHAPTER 4 *Quote: "Do We just Yield...?"*

I had not followed the nuance of his humor, nor had I understood his reply, so I simply said, "Yes." I had not been aware, but now I suddenly became so, that an entire British entourage was listening in. Laughter broke out like thunder throughout the whole room, with the exception of our table. There we sat, serious like little Popes, not understanding. There was a gentleman who, having picked up on these goings-on, came over. Most graciously he explained to us what the terms meant. At last it was our turn to guffaw, and the rest of the evening was gay, lubricated by a profusion of good wine.

*   *   *

Our little group of six went out often together. One evening at a different restaurant, an unforeseen incident, which might have become serious trouble, produced roars of laughter from all those present... except for me. I wasn't sure if I should be furious or join in the energetic laughter of the group.

Tables were generally squeezed pretty tightly together, as these restaurants were typically full. Truth be told, tables seemed to be one on top of the other. We were bouncing stories back and forth as we were waiting to be served. At the next table, the one just behind me, which was very noisy by the way, one guy hopped up so quickly that he toppled the waiter's cargo. This waiter was in the process of squeezing past with a tray which he carried on one wide-open hand, and the tray supported a full pot of soup! No missing me: the soup found its mark and coiffed me ever so effectively. Thank goodness the soup was not boiling hot, but there I sat with soup running all down my uniform, sticky noodles for hair and a room full of onlookers, who joined in resounding laughter. Today, I can look back and laugh, but not then. The waiter was embarrassed and apologetic, yet after all it was not his fault.

Right away the manager showed up, embarrassed in his own way but mainly looking to verify I hadn't been hurt. He took me into his office and loaned me some wearing apparel while the staffers took great care in cleaning my uniform, with a thousand polite British apologies. Conclusion? We all got the reward of a sumptuous meal at no cost, irrigated by the best of free wine, and the manager nonetheless thanked us for having chosen his establishment.

*   *   *

Lieutenant Colonel Pijeaud was in charge of the Free French soldiers at the Saint Athan base, and arriving at this base the men were questioned as to their knowledge of English. Those who had a good working knowledge of the language were sent to training centers alongside Royal Air Force pilots. The others, I included, were expected to learn it, especially technical terms like the ones pertaining to weapons, instruments in the cockpit, and motors. The idea was to get us through test-taking as soon as possible, then on to standard R.A.F. training.

I was soon accepted for flight training on the Mile Magistaire, a trainer aircraft which was pretty spacious inside. It is not to be confused with Miles Master which is a similar model that's more powerful and appropriate for real aerobatics. My acceptance for this training told me I was making good progress with my English, and at the Saint Athan base many of us were studying with good results. Having flown for four weeks, my English tested ok, and as promised I was allowed to study side by side with advanced students. There were Belgians, Poles and the French from the *Trébouliste*. To name a few of my "grand escape" companions, there were Maurice Vergès, René Moine, a Mr. Duperrier, Jean Godin and Gonzalès Caron.

The city of Odiham, in Berkshire, was the "I.T.W." Center, or Initial Training Wing, for the Royal Air Force. These "Miles" airplanes had been specifically designed for high power combat training, and these planes intimidated me a bit. Just as with any plane, a guy took the stick with caution at first. Patience, perseverance and mastery of the dynamics of this bird were to go hand in hand with my determination to succeed. My British instructors took great satisfaction at the way I performed on my exams.

Next step: Ternhill, England. I earned my "wing" again, this time from the R.A.F. My hope and dream was to go fly with the Alsace Fighter Group or some other combat squadron, perhaps of the R.A.F.

Some very good news had come to us via Lieutenant Pinot: we would be able to continue our student pilot training and at the same time get paid. Our families would be compensated, too, in the event of an accident.

Vera, my fiancée, age 20

A few months after voluntarily
enlisting: Private Drabier

War Pilot Memoirs: A Mirror on 1939

CHAPTER 5

Deployed to Arabia

*Our insignia was the one which eventually became the best loved out of all the Free French Forces. That metallic wing on the chest became well known and popular with all the guys. In the first days of the war, the Free French Air Force was at Saint Athan, England, under the command of Major Lalouette. At the beginning, what the flyboys put on their uniforms was the mariners' blue diamond-shaped background with a cross of Lorraine, but soon enough the aviators of the Free French Forces wanted their own insignia. General de Gaulle being down in Africa, the responsible parties made this desire known to Major Lalouette, who was receptive to the idea. He forwarded the idea to Admiral Muselier who took on the job.

The Cross of Lorraine

In his General Order Number Two of 03 JULY 1940 {two weeks after the *Trébouliste* had transported us to England}, Admiral Émile Muselier {1882-1965, age 58 at the time}, who two days earlier had been appointed commander of the Naval and Airborne Free French Forces, established, for all French fighters rallying under de Gaulle, the insignia *Pavillon de Beaupré*. This was a blue, four-sided diamond shape that bore, in the center, a red cross of Lorraine, which was meant to show opposition to the Germans' twisted cross shaped like

*Excerpt from *Les Forces Aériennes Françaises Libres*, page 140 {Amicale des FAFL, 52 rue Vergniaud, Paris 75013}

capital gammas in Greek. By the same General Order, airplanes got emblems {round or oval or shaped like a shield} with the cross of Lorraine in the center. The insignia for the uniforms got modified two months later because it was too dark. In the final version it was, in order from the outside in: blue, white, red. The white was the diamond shape and it bore a red cross of Lorraine, with its two crossbars but without knobs on the ends.

#   #   #

As soon as Lalouette got back to the base at Saint Athan, England, he asked enlisted man **Jacques Drabier**, age 18, student from The Beaux-arts School in Paris, to draw an insignia which should include one star above outstretched wings, which had been the emblem of the Air Corps, plus a shield with the national colors, plus the cross of Lorraine, plus the letters F.A.F.L. for *Forces Aériennes Françaises Libres*. Heeding his request, {I drew}* several sketches and the best one was submitted to headquarters in London, which gave its approval on the condition that it also be sent to Admiral Muselier.

The Admiral, then, wound up wearing the Free French Air Force emblem underneath the cross of Lorraine belonging to the Free French Naval Forces. The cross of Lorraine {region of far eastern France near Germany} is often called "the cross of Anjou" {region of western France, southwest of Paris} or the "cross of Anjou-Lorraine." It is found, from 1473 onward, in the emblems of the Dukes of Lorraine.

The coat of arms displayed by Joan of Arc in the early 1400s was an azure shield with two *fleurs de lys* (lilies) and, in the middle, a sword. {I was}* inspired, then, by the azure shield, both by its shape and its color, yet in the center {I eliminated}* the two golden *fleurs de lys*, symbols of royalty, as I replaced the sword with the cross of Lorraine. Based on this, then, {I visualized}* in short order the rest of the composition: 1) wings which support us, 2) the star which guides us, 3) the shield, emblem of our liberty with its cross of Lorraine, and 4) the national colors of France shown obliquely. Underneath is the banner emblazoned with the letters F.A.F.L. The

---

* I hereby verify the accuracy of the other writer; in his article the words are "Drabier" or "he."

CHAPTER 5 *Deployed to Arabia*

official insignia of the Free French Air Force was given to all those who had joined from July of 1940. This continued until August of 1943 when our Air Force returned to the regular insignia.

It was not until October of 1940 that production started with a first run of two hundred. These were struck by a Mr. Campbell, jeweler of the Brompton Arcade in London. The first run items were numbered, then issued to individuals in chronological order, as best could be done. This was based on the dates when individuals had joined and based on their rank in the Air Corps. Number one (1) went to General de Gaulle when he got back from Africa, #2 went to Admiral Muselier, #3 to Colonel Pijeaud who commanded the Free French Air Force while it was in England, #4 to Major Lalouette.

A detail in the placement of the French shield is noteworthy. The national colors are not displayed vertically as per custom. They are diagonal for esthetic reasons, matching the attractive esthetics of certain flags and emblems of the French Revolution and of the First {year 1804} and Second {1852} Empires.

#   #   #

General de Gaulle reviewed the troops at Saint Athan in the week prior to Bastille Day, 1940, which fell on a Sunday that year. Revolutionaries in 1789 attacked the Bastille prison, a symbol of the former regime, so we celebrate the 14th of July. I am proud to have been among the troops that Charles de Gaulle reviewed, as I have been proud to deem myself a Gaullist. Another famous figure admired by pilots of my era was Antoine de St. Exupery, a war pilot and an author, well known for <u>The Little Prince</u>. As to when he visited our base, I cannot say, but I recall how he buzzed on through as if a man on a definitive mission and how he had a good number of staffers following him. Even the German pilots were reading his writings, so it took over fifty years for the one who shot him down to admit it, as detailed in a very good book* which I recommend.

* *ST-EXUPÉRY L'ULTIME SECRET,* Pradel + Vanrell, www.EditionsDuRocher.fr 2008.

Saturday 13 JULY 1940. General de Gaulle,
by radio over the British Broadcasting Corporation:
"Tonight, on the eve of Bastille Day,
there is not one Frenchman or Frenchwoman
who is not focused on the needs of France.
Do not go thinking we should plunge ourselves into depression
or give in to resignation,
for any such sad abandonment would play into the hands
of our enemies.
Our Motherland, divided as she may be, pillaged as she may be,
even given, in part, to the enemy as she may be,
must not play the role of one defeated.
And so, given that certain persons whose duty it was
to wield the sword of France
have dropped it… and broken it… I myself
have picked up the shattered blade.
I am pleased to announce that there already exists
an appreciable military force under my command, and
that it is ready to strike on a moment's notice
by land, by air and by sea.
Moreover, this force is growing every day, and
I want it known that the youth of France possesses
a magnificent caliber and
is rallying to engage in the fight.
Not even for a moment may you doubt
that this force will rise to the level necessary for war.
Frenchman, Frenchwoman, know it:
you indeed still have a combat army!
If the 14th of July, 1940, is a day of sorrow
for the Motherland, it must
at the same time be a sunny day of stubborn faith
in all things good.
Yes, we will bring victory home, and
so it must be!
My endless source of help is
the armed forces of France."

*   *   *

CHAPTER 5   *Deployed to Arabia*

One day my commander, Colonel Charles Pijeaud, called me into his office. A respected man, a tall, dark and striking figure of a man, the *colonel* [in French, pronounce ko-lo-NELL] had to travel far and wide for the establishing of various units. These units were to participate in combat under the auspices of the Royal Air Force of England. When I say "his office" then, picture an improvised one; this was the norm. The city was Odiham, England, and I had just come in from flying a Hurricane, a British fighter. I needed to log hours since I wanted to be assigned to a combat group.

Colonel Pijeaud received me very graciously, and he asked me if everything was going ok. I explained how eager I was to get assigned. Looking me in the eye, he said, "How many of you French pilots are still waiting?"

I replied, "Oh, a bunch of us have already gone. There's only four or five now."

He told me, "Assemble your colleagues. I want all of you here in a half hour. I may have some good news for you guys." All I could think was "cool" as I ran to get my buddies. We were militarily punctual in presenting ourselves, five of us in all.

"Flight instructors are needed in the Middle East," Colonel Pijeaud announced to us. He went on to say how flyovers to survey the Syrian desert required pilots too. Both Syria and Lebanon had recently been liberated, so Generals de Gaulle and Montgomery had decided that these two countries, having been French protectorates prior to the war, should become part of the overseas military operation of the Free French.

It was up to us, then, to go about purifying these regions infested with Germans, who were supporting the local tribes in sabotaging pipelines. These important pipelines crossed the Syrian desert from Baghdad, Iraq, to the city of Tripoli on the Mediterranean coast of Lebanon, where ships took on the oil.

All the while watching us for a reaction, and without further commentary, Colonel Pijeaud used his finger toward each of us, Maurice Vergès, René Moine, Ducorneau, me and the fifth guy too, saying, "Messieurs, you are going to Damascus, Syria, and I'll give you 48 hours to get ready. A convoy is pulling out this week, and you'll be in it."

Once out of sight of the Colonel, our mouths dropped open over this unpleasant surprise. We certainly never expected the Middle* East. The fighting was finished in Syria, this being late 1941, and there was surely not a dogfight to be had!

Our basic reaction was "what a dirty trick" to play on us! We were furious with Colonel Pijeaud and none too happy with the whole scheme of things, yet we were just subordinates. Better not to utter a word, having no choice in the matter, so we took his decision as final. Setting aside my anger, my dismay, I tried to think of it as a case where maybe the Colonel knew better than we did what was important.

Today when I think of Colonel Pijeaud, I feel emotions of esteem and respect. He soon left England to command the Lorraine Fighter Group. While the five of us were on our way to Damascus, he was flying a bomber on a mission to attack German columns near the Mediterranean port city of Benghazi, Libya, in North Africa. Escorted by Allied fighters, they faced an attack by numerous enemy fighters who had the advantage of altitude. There was one terrible bloodbath and many planes went down. The plane that Colonel Pijeaud was flying got hit hard. One of its motors caught fire which caused it to lose altitude fast. The navigator parachuted out, I think, but as Colonel Pijeaud was preparing to jump, he noticed the machine-gunner still at his post, not knowing the poor guy was already dead. Instead of jumping, the Colonel landed the doomed plane, by the grace of God since his landing gear was not deployed.

Colonel Pijeaud was severely burned, and he was captured by the Italians there in Libya as he tried to flee. Transported across the Mediterranean to a hospital in the city of Alexandria, near Turin in northwest Italy, he succumbed to his injuries in this hospital. What an end for a brave man, who simply tried to save the

---

*My logbooks carry official seals saying "*Moyen-Orient*" for "Middle East", even though some people say "Near East."

CHAPTER 5 *Deployed to Arabia*

life of his machine-gunner, who was already done for, at the risk of his own life. The date of his death is reported as 6 January 1942, so he was 37 years old.

A long sea voyage lay ahead of us, the fated five guys who had just left Colonel Pijeaud's presence there in 1941. It would take us all the way down beyond Cape Town, South Africa, then up along the coast of Madagascar to reach the port of Ismalia, Egypt. From there it's a short distance to Damascus. News traveled slowly too, so I learned of the Colonel's demise as we passed through Cairo, Egypt.

Free French Air Force insignia,
Cross of Lorraine = freedom

St. Athan, England 7/7/1940
I am in the middle.

War Pilot Memoirs: A Mirror on 1939

CHAPTER 6

Anti-sabotage by Camelback, Improvised Bombs

Syria
I get Stationed at Damascus

Late January, 1942, saw my comrades and me at Cairo. From Egypt, a convoy of military trucks took us off to Syria. Oh, the backbreaking jarring from so many so-called roads where rocks were more plentiful than sand. We made stops as frequently as we could, seeking an oasis whenever possible since that was a perfect place to "break bread together", to have some chow. These oases were distinguishable from a great distance, given their palm trees, which were loaded with green dates. The trees stood in circles amidst endless miles of sand, and it was there that you'd find drinking water. On rare occasions we had the good fortune to feed upon fresh meat, usually gazelle meat. The meats of the Muslim Bedouins were lamb and gazelle, and they called it *machwi*, serving it up as a shish kabob on a bed of couscous.

The trip took us a day and a half. By good luck we met up with a camel convoy, nomadic Arab merchants who had set up camp for the night. By means of trading, well, truly bribing and cajoling which included some money in addition to some surplus supplies we had of blankets and such, we convinced these nomads to share their immense tents with us. Big tents they were, assembled from several pieces since just one camel couldn't possibly have carried the weight of one tent. These merchants had family members traveling with them, yet all forty soldiers – two truckloads worth – found refuge. What a stroke of luck it was since the winds blew like beating propellers that evening. When darkness fell, a sandstorm whipped in. This was all so new to us European kids, yet soon enough we learned the tricks of how to protect ourselves. Your eyes were what needed protecting the most, and the simple concept of keeping your mouth shut let you avoid swallowing the obvious yet inevitable sand. Communicating with each other while your mouth was both closed and wrapped up in a scarf? Well, you learned.

Awake at sunrise, the spectacle that we saw was impressive: in what you'll picture as a "winter wonderland", absolutely everything was covered in sand. Our trucks we had to dig out, scrape off and wipe down. While we went about this work, one of us commented, "Where the heck are the camels?" We could see little mounds of sand, but not one single camel, when suddenly the little mounds took to vibrating. Out popped our precious camels, as they set themselves to shaking off sand. These camels emitted an ear-piercing noise, but I can also say it resembled the plaintive baying of a hound dog.

After much effort we got moving again. All you saw was sand, sand and more sand. We crossed from what is now Israel into Syria. As we made for Damascus, some Kurds came alongside to escort us. They were really acting as French soldiers. They were there to survey and maintain safety in the Syrian desert, which stretches from the Iraqi frontier in the east to the doorway of the Mediterranean which is Lebanon in the west. Their surveillance was crucial since hundreds of miles of pipeline, bringing oil out of Iraq, lay there unprotected.

These nomadic warriors were friends to the French, who in recompense furnished them foodstuffs and protection as these nomads participated in Free French military operations. The

CHAPTER 6   *Anti-sabotage by Camelback, Improvised Bombs*

French Foreign Legion was there too. There did exist some Arabs who collaborated with the Germans, and these groups would blow up pipelines and conduct other acts of sabotage.

Here we were now in the city of Damascus. It is home to the Umayyad Mosque, one of the biggest mosques in all the Muslim world, having ninety gold domes. This was a fabulous sight, yet an overwhelming sight when the sunshine came beaming down, reflecting in all directions. Our base of operations near the city of Damascus was our final stop, and we could start to unwind. I was here to serve as Monitor-Instructor attached to the Mixed Instruction Group, our *G.M.I., Groupe mixte d'instruction*, the word "mixed" being used to show that we trained new pilots in addition to flying war missions. An Instructor, of course, was a teacher, whereas a Monitor was one who flew "second chair" for reasons of control.

The base commander, Major Noël, received us upon arrival. Our barracks were two-story buildings, and after stowing our gear we were shown around the Headquarters. Walking the aircraft operations area came next, where I found the hangars... well, the hangar... to be surprisingly sparse. All I could see were two Potez 25s, one Simoun-Caudron, one Farman and one Stamp. I did not dare to inquire out loud, but where the heck were the airplanes? Being the new kid on the block, I guarded my tongue. Off we went to chow, where we met Adjutant Huin*, Chief Ballatore and Sergeant Mallard. Each of them presented himself as a Monitor-Instructor. We were prematurely happy when they offered us a glass of hospitality; we clinked a toast, but, yuk, what the devil was this? *Arak*. It was like the strongest moonshine you can imagine or a sample of *pastis* out of Provence at ten times its strength. Wow, you had to pay attention to drink it, and hope it had been well chilled. On the second glass, a guy could still stay vertical, but watch out for the third! You would fall like a deflating crepe on the plate.

---

* rhymes with Chopin; pronounce hue-Î, but omitting the initial "h"

I was still sipping slowly on my glass of *arak* when the Adjutant asked me which airplanes I had flown. Proudly I touted the list of British planes I had piloted, plus the Lucioles and the Moranes from my earlier time at Morlaix in the French region of Brittany. Smiling, he said to me, "That's great. We'll be putting you in a Potez [pronounce '-ez' to rhyme with 'says'] Twenty-five and I will personally be your monitor."

Taken somewhat aback, I replied, "Huh? Is this a joke?" Having flown Hurricanes, this would be like going from a sleek sports car to an oxcart.

"Begging your pardon," he said, "no joke. For the time being that's all we have. The Brits have been promising better planes for a long time, but nothing yet. Our Hurricanes have motor stalls all the time. The never-ending Syrian wind blows sand into the Hurricanes' motors, so we've got them parked. Only the Potez 25 can eat just as much sand as gasoline, and she doesn't even cough. Besides, she's perfect to use as a trainer, for supplies that need to be flown in, for surveillance and aerial photography. And she lands in the sand like she was born to it."

I followed his reasoning. I asked him what weapons "she" carried for this surveillance, and the answer was two .30-caliber machineguns, that is to say with bullets smaller than in a .38 revolver, plus about ten little two-pound bombs or "antipersonnel bombs" mounted under the wings. Hmm, ok. When do we start?

Adjutant Huin served me up another glass of *arak*, saying, "Weather permitting, tomorrow."

*   *   *

By sunrise the next morning I was in my seat onboard a Potez 25. Since it was a trainer with dual controls, my seat was up front and the monitor's was behind me. Off we went. We made it an impromptu reconnaissance mission, having no particular maneuvers to perform. We were at an altitude of fifteen hundred feet, flying toward Damascus, when I discovered that the Syrian sun

CHAPTER 6 *Anti-sabotage by Camelback, Improvised Bombs*

had no pity for a newly arrived European. It was March, 1942, so the heat was not too intense this early in the year; this was a blessing.

An extremely bright object suddenly became visible out there, just about the time we could see Damascus on the horizon. Between me and my monitor, Huin, communications were via telephonic tube. Through this tube you really had to holler to overcome the whistling noise of wind on the cables. Both student pilot and instructor were out in the open air on this plane: nothing but a little windshield to deflect the air. Those little leather caps and hard glass goggles were never more appreciated. I asked my monitor what in the world that was, that brilliant reflection of the sun way over there. Its radiance was intense, the sun being behind us and shining on the reflection source up ahead. He explained that it was the Umayyad Mosque with its gold domes in all their glory. He further explained that if I ever found myself lost in flight in the desert, this would be my reference point. "They're always shining," he told me, "except at night." Even more spectacular was the God's eye view when we flew directly above them. We were only about six hundred feet up, and wow!

Well, here we were, back above our own base, where we touched down like a pair of aces. I started thinking to myself this really wasn't a bad piece of machinery, this Potez 25 (named for a Monsieur Potez): open cockpits, single small engine. It was manageable, accommodating, easy to maneuver... I was starting to feel a bond.

*   *   *

Now June of 1942 and the sun was enough to knock you out, but you had to get used to it because here, you see, we flew in any weather conditions. We had taught ourselves to go nowhere without a canteen. One particular morning I was with several instructors when we walked past the "very old airplane" hangar. One of these planes was a 1932 *Bloch 81 sanitaire*, configured for carrying the injured. Boy she did evermore show her age:

square fuselage, fabric-covered wings mounted high and, just like on a canal boat, those windows, round like portholes, which really dated her. I looked at my monitor, saying, "Still airworthy, this footlocker?"

He cracked a smile, replying, "Oh, yes. If we need an ambulance for air-evac, we use it, so we keep it up and running. Drabier, you're going to fly it with weaponry instructor Quesnel." This Sergeant Quesnel was right there with us.

Adjutant Huin, his finger pointing at me, said that I had the Potez 25 so much under my belt that I'd have no trouble with this Bloch 81. We got help from several mechanics to roll the old girl out of the hangar. I donned my parachute, we climbed inside, and the head mechanic turned the prop by hand to get the motor started. There were no dual controls in this old puppy, so the pilot's seat alone hugged up to the dashboard. Two seats, just behind the pilot and to his right, faced sideways, and on the opposite side of the fuselage there was room for a stretcher or for cargo. Surprised that this configuration would be used for training, for teaching us how to shoot, I queried Sergeant Quesnel, the weaponry instructor. This old airplane, lightweight and capable of really slow airspeeds, was best for towing the wind sock that the guys would fire upon. Ah, I was starting to grasp the concept.

As we taxied onto the runway I noticed a strange characteristic in this set of controls: the "broomstick" main control was mounted from the ceiling, and so was the lever that controlled fuel to the motor. This nuisance of a configuration is and was unique in my experience. You had to be careful if you had your arm up there at the same time you needed to look left. This meant peeking over or under your own arm, and it was dangerous.

Finally we took off, and luckily the wind was not too strong. You see, about thirty-five miles an hour was all the speed you needed to take off, so if you were rolling into a forty-five mph wind you'd actually be able to take off rolling backwards! Anyway, this flying box-crate was an experience to add to my list, but the next day I woke up happy to be back onboard my Potez 25.

CHAPTER 6   *Anti-sabotage by Camelback, Improvised Bombs*

Fifty flight hours I put in on this bird, the Potez 25, with every imaginable landing scenario, including nighttime operations and including landing on raw sand in contrast to tarmac or concrete. On some of these Potez 25s you had a machine-gunner's seat behind the pilot and the machinegun was on a turnstile. The little antipersonnel bombs were mounted under the lower wings, and funny as they were to look at, you didn't want to fool around. Let me explain.

The mechanism we used for releasing these bombs was simple, yet precarious. Steel wires, which were thin like picture-hanging wire, went from each bomb to a hook underneath the dashboard. The hooks were neatly arranged above your knees and the release handles or "pull tabs" were the simple mechanical type you'd yank out by hand. One yank on a handle was engineered to release two bombs at a time, one from the left wing and one from the right. My take on this was to parallel it to the most archaic of medieval weapons, and as to accuracy, well, I won't even go there. You'd have had a better chance of hitting something if you had tossed the bombs out by hand, like a kid throwing rocks.

Let's not criticize too severely my little Potez 25. She served me really well and flew us home after many a successful mission thanks to the skill and zeal of my machine-gunner Tauzi. Later on, Tauzi, a fellow Frenchman, was assigned to me as a photographer. Our photo missions and the missions of others there at the base drew plenty of attention from Headquarters. They honored our surveillance group with a name, *Groupe de surveillance Picardie*. From then on, you see, we'd function under better military protocol with official briefings, plus now we'd fly with the cross of Lorraine painted on our planes.

Oil pipelines came out of Baghdad, Iraq, and crossed the whole Syrian desert before traversing the mountains of Lebanon to reach Tripoli, a huge Lebanese seaport on the Mediterranean. The Spahi and the Druze tribes surveyed the region on horseback and camelback, but some other tribes were sabotaging Allied efforts because they got paid by the Germans.

The immensity of the desert surface area rendered horses and camels less than effective. A "No Man Zone" was established by F.A.F.L. Headquarters, being a strip of land with its boundaries four miles on either side of the pipeline stretching for a good three hundred miles in length. Anyone seen in No Man's Land was tracked, and on occasion violators were fired upon without warning. It was war; we had the right.

There were secondary airstrips at places like Palmyra and Balbek where we would touch down, just to stretch our legs or have a smoke. Little airbases like this had been placed about twenty miles apart. I recall an intriguing historical monument at Balbek in the form of immense columns. This marked, for me, how my noble predecessors, the Romans, had passed through two thousand years earlier. Over at Palmyra, Syria, you saw little dwellings dating to an earlier era of Turkish control, closer to three thousand years ago.

Both marvelous and extraordinary, if these ruins could talk, I can only imagine the stories they'd tell. How many of my predecessors had gathered dates from these date palms? I happen to love dates, and I ate my fill. Off on the horizon I'd see gazelles leaping. These animals could zigzag gracefully, even at forty miles an hour, a trick which made them hard to hunt. The Muslims of the region ate neither pork nor chicken, so they'd try to capture or kill gazelles, without much success. Thus it was that these tribal people had very little meat in their diet.

On a routine patrolling mission one day in the desert, onboard my precious Potez 25, suddenly I heard misfires in the motor. The coughing was incessant. Then the motor just flat out shut down. "Be calm. No cause for alarm." Tauzi, my machine-gunner, was with me. I was not only trained for this but accustomed to it, so I glided in for a sandy landing with no trouble. The heat was absolutely torrid, easily a hundred and twenty Fahrenheit but with not even a tickle of a wind. When you fly, the air might be hot but it's moving.

We looked around: not a sign of life. Tauzi radioed an S.O.S.

CHAPTER 6   *Anti-sabotage by Camelback, Improvised Bombs*

to the base to get them to send someone to affect repair, explaining it was the carburetor. By rudimentary "nose length" reconnoitering, he gave our position. There was an oasis a quarter-mile away, so he gave this oasis as a reference point.

We started walking toward the oasis, not just to kill time but really to lubricate our throats, yet one always had a certain curiosity. The tribal people that received us were called Touaregues and though they weren't militarized, they were pro-French. From an operations standpoint, this tribe generally helped us know what was going on around their villages and this was particularly beneficial at night. The Kaïd, or chief of the tribe, hosted us in his tent, making the sign with his right hand motioning away from his forehead then touching his chest then opening toward the right, which meant "welcome", *Allah salamek*!

It was surprisingly comfortable for temperature in these tents. The "moo-kaires" (women) offered us water with which to wash our hands before they served us a very aromatic tea in these little cups. We explained how our airplane was broken down and that we had sent out a call for help. We expected the help to arrive within two hours.

While we waited, we heard the Touaregue women talk about life in general and complain about the lack of meat. Their husbands told us how they could not successfully hunt gazelles. In the course of conversation, I made, or perhaps Tauzi made, an offer to help them get some gazelle meat on the table. This prompted wide-eyed stares directed at us, with, "Allah. Allah is just. But how can you do this?" These Arabs were very superstitious, and receiving a gift absolutely meant offering a gift. But what did they have to offer? After what I could see to be careful reflection, they told us they wanted to offer us some two-liter bottles of rum. Truth be told, they didn't know what to do with it otherwise, since they didn't drink alcohol. It had been given to them by other military personnel. Now what do you think of that?

So we accepted. Abruptly our dear Kaïd opened his eyes big and wide, all the while preening his scraggly beard, and said,

"Ha! How can you do it? You not run fast enough," as he burst into laughter.

Among the wealthier tribes there was a system for hunting gazelles that involved dogs, little sand-colored Arabian dogs, built like greyhounds, called "sloughis." At first glance they look enough like a European dog, but their paws are elongated and narrow. They were renowned for fast running on the sand so they could chase the gazelles back toward the tribesmen, who would shoot the game. Sadly neither we nor the Kaïd had any sloughis.

Suddenly, above our heads we saw a Potez 25 and the pilot was surely verifying we were there. He buzzed over at low altitude, spotted us and gave signals with his wings that he had seen us. He landed close to our disabled airplane. The mechanic hopped out with his toolbox and spare parts. I recognized one of my former monitors, Sergeant Mollard, who hollered out, "Well, boys, what in the world is going on?" We shook hands. He politely responded to the Kaïd's salutation of *salamek* and we were again ushered into the big tent. We told Mollard the story of how we had negotiated an exchange of gazelle meat for rum. Smiling, he said to me, "Alright. You're the one who made the promise. Take my plane and bring these people back a gazelle."

Gazelle Hunting

Tauzi accompanied me. We took off and quickly enough found a herd of gazelles. I flew us low. Tauzi was at the ready, his eye on the gun sight of his machinegun. Of course we were faster than the gazelles. There, we had one alongside: pow pow, pow pow. We flew over as the poor beast rolled, then lay flat, dead where he fell. He never had a chance. We made a loop to come back and land near where the beast lay. This one was big, too heavy to put in the plane, so we had to field dress him, which took a good half hour. The hide is precious too, providing leather to these nomads for sandals and for bedcovers.

We took our bounty back to the tribe, they who had been watch-

CHAPTER 6   *Anti-sabotage by Camelback, Improvised Bombs*

ing from a distance. They were dancing, singing, giving off that unique blubbering percussion sound they made with their fingers and their lips. This was an unusual display of emotion, but we clearly knew how happy they were to have meat, and it would last a good while. Joy was radiating from their faces.

In the meantime the mechanic had replaced the defective carburetor in our Potez, and her motor was just purring. We were proud of our exploits, proud to have helped our tribal colleagues, but prouder yet to show up among our French pilots group with nine or ten bottles of rum. "Comrades at arms: cheers!"

*   *   *

I finally had this Potez 25 really and truly under my belt. Since it was in the cards that I should become an instructor, I worked hard at it. Training included flying at high altitude, navigating, descending in a spiral, swerving with or without propeller power, and landing with the motor off. Realize that this model of airplane did not allow you to restart the motor in flight once it was stopped. It was really important, then, to know not only how to land but how to find a spot to land. To be avoided at all cost was to hit the ground short of the landing zone, as this could easily flip your plane over onto its back. In addition, we used the word "piqué" for landing too steeply. Both these events caused much damage during the war and many a mortal wound.

Long flight hours were required before you even attempted full speed landings on a shortened field. Moreover, you had your P.S.V. training, for *pilotage sans visibilité* which means blind flying! You had to be certified, and my certificate is dated 5 May 1943, a curious fact in itself since I had already received my wings from the Royal Air Force. This was nothing nefarious or bizarre, just an administrative flip-flop. Anyway, I was now a full fledged fighter pilot, allowed to wear the *macaron de pilote français*, pilot's wings on my chest.

Surveillance Group

Photographic missions were important to the war effort, and I was sent on many of them. Reconnaissance missions appear in my flight log in the two weeks leading up to Christmas, on 14DEC1942 and on 23DEC1942. The cities photographed were Es Souïeda, Ezraa and Damascus itself. Among certain tribes, there had been movement which was unclear to us. Likewise we flew a photographic mission over Khan el Koura where, even though we were unarmed, we got shot at. There was a group of camouflaged trucks, each one full of enemy soldiers. We radioed, and sure enough there arrived a whole group of Potez 25s armed with machineguns and bombs. They did what was called for, and the enemy troops scattered under fire.

Meanwhile, roughly two hundred student pilots showed up from Algeria. Oh, these Potez 25s were starting to show their age with all this work. We queried Beirut Headquarters: when, oh when, are we going to get some new planes?

My sketch of the Touaregues' tent.
Our Potez 25 broke down near here.

War Pilot Memoirs: A Mirror on 1939

CHAPTER 7

Bristol-Blenheims, those old *Potez* and American Monocoupes

Along came a miracle: the ninety horsepower Monocoupe from the U.S. of A. It had two wings, not four. It was deceptively innocent-looking, this four-seater, in that it could perform far better as a war plane than appearances led you to believe.

Monocoupe (Franklin Company, USA)

Thirty-three Monocoupes, model 90AF, were produced in 1941 and duly commissioned as civilian aircraft in the United States. With a remarkable lack of civilian clients, they became warplanes, even carrying bombs. Twenty of the thirty-three were sent to the Free French Air Force in the Middle East. These were used in our flight schools and for our Air Corps on military missions. Some reports tell of our young men's "thirst" for aviation, yet, as attractive a description as this may be, I'm here to tell our story in a slightly different light.

Brass tacks is brass tacks, which is a way to say how important simple rudiments are to military operations. These Monocoupes just had to be retrofitted with some way to fight off the desert sand. I've read that the U.S. Army Air Corps insisted that the planes be equipped with sand-resistant air filters, and that they wouldn't even sign a contract otherwise. Used for hundreds of missions, this little dinky plane carried a bomb weighing a hundred and ten pounds. Reports are that it was used by the Americans to attack U-Boats.

Once the excitement among our Free French squadrons wore off a bit, we found ourselves blessed with some useable machinery. We had been flying, among others, the twin-engine Blenheim, and our* Surveillance Squadron of Eastern Mediterranean States, created 16NOV1942, had a disparate set of machines, namely Potez 63s, Blenheims and Potez 25s. This squadron was under the command of Captain Guigonis. The very first new model for us, a red and beige Monocoupe #NC38920, arrived at the city of Damascus in February, 1943, on the very same day the daughter of Captain Guigonis was being baptized. Her name was Mireille, and the child's name got painted onto the front of the airplane.

These Monocoupes were welcomed at the city of Rayack, Lebanon, also. Right off, we set ourselves to studying this little plane of innocent demeanor. Well, "innocent" was not exactly the right adjective. She was very sensitive to commands from the controls, her "fletching", her feathers, her ailerons being undersized in comparison to her long fuselage. At slow airspeeds, things got really delicate. All things considered, though, that little sparrow brought this flight instructor out of many a thunderstorm.

By February of 1943, at age 20, I was showing I knew how to handle myself in flight. On Tuesday, February 9th, by my flight log, instructor Cornez decided to try me out in a twin-engine Blenheim IV, so I climbed into the front seat as he took the dual control seat as monitor. I performed just fine, and all he said after our flight was, "Be a little more vigilant. Pay attention to your instruments."

On Saturday, February 13th, 1943, Chief Adjutant Ballatore took me up in a Morane Saulnier 230 to see me perform aerobatics like 360s, which we called *boucle renversée* for "the upside down buckle." I also did spiraling pirouettes in a climb, and after this I remember how my tummy was squirming.

* *Escadrille de Surveillance des Territoires des Etats du Levant;* see magazine <u>Le Fana de l'Aviation</u>, Sept. 2000: *"Les petits oiseaux* {little birds} *de la France Libre"*

CHAPTER 7 *Bristol-Blenheims...*

During the month of March, 1943, I did a lot of flying in the Potez 25. I had to get used to being without visibility in preparation for teaching. Finally they put me into a Monocoupe. Captain Guigonis said to me, "We'll be needing to master every nuance of that one, the way a lion tamer masters a lion." He knew the Monocoupe was going to serve us well for training, for missions, for transport including mail and for medical evacuations. Monocoupe #38912, with dual controls, was assigned to me. Once up in the air I perceived a certain lightness, a certain ease of command, but while setting her back down I found myself shuffling my feet pretty frantically, nervous little plane that she was. You couldn't really use the brakes on the wheels for fear of poking the nose into the ground.

On Wednesday, March 17th, I found myself up in my Monocoupe wanting to train diligently, especially to get quicker at shuffling my feet. As a nice gesture to Tauzi, I had taken him along, and in my logbook it's spelled "Tauzy." When you carried a passenger beside you in this plane you removed the control handle on the right so the passenger's feet didn't interfere with operations. This "broomstick" was simply a tube and there was a stowage clip overhead.

Flying double-commands ("D/C"), I often took Maurice Vergès along, likewise Sergeant Jean Ducorneaux, who soon became an instructor himself, or René Moine. But it was Tauzi who really got a kick out of flying with me, since he had this ambition of becoming an *observateur* on twin-engine planes, that is to say the guy who sighted through the bomb sight. Our school now possessed four Monocoupes, so I flew each, in rotation, to assure they stayed in good working order. Numbers 20 and 32 were often used by Captain Guigonis.

On Thursday, May 6th, 1943, I flew Monocoupe #12 for a navigation mission. It was the first time I had taken a Monocoupe, abbreviated "MP" in our flight logs, on a long distance flight. This one was Damascus to Sazzera-Deir-Aeli to Damascus, a round trip of fifty minutes.

On Friday, May 14th, we were teamed up as four pilots. I was flying Monocoupe #20 and my colleagues flew the other three. We had no trouble, delicate as it was, flying wing tip to wing tip. There is a certain pilot's confidence of togetherness which comes from this. It is akin to military discipline, yet different.

Later the same day the loudspeaker called me up to go bring back a pilot who'd broken down with carburetor trouble, and I took Monocoupe #12. A mechanic named Granc and I took off from Damascus for Sbeine, where we landed on the sand with no damage to us or the aircraft. Pilots in training under me needed a certain number of flight hours to graduate to other aircraft, so I was up in a Monocoupe plenty often.

May – June 1943: training to fly in tight formation. On the last day of May, I flew Lieutenant Barbier round trip to Beirut. I had the luxury of admiring the beaches of Lebanon. The duration was 1 hour 55 minutes each way. June – July 1943, I was back in my Potez 25 flying missions, since mine was the only Potez that was equipped with a machinegun.

A little rubric appears in the magazine Fana de l'Aviation, #370, September, 2000. The title is "Missions of War." It was a pleasant experience to see myself cited:

> Damascus became more and more the operations center for relay missions, where official documents got passed along as if a baton in a relay race, and for observation missions. The task of schooling was little by little moved to Rayack, Lebanon, thirty-five miles to the northwest. The Monocoupes of Rayack got called out more and more to affect surveillance of the pipeline bringing petroleum from Baghdad, Iraq, to Tripoli, Lebanon. These Monocoupes flew the same missions as the Potez 25s, which were fitted with either a camera or a machinegun, and the missions included surveying Arabic tribes seen as belligerent. With this double activity of pipeline and tribal surveillance increasing in frequency, the number of planes soon became

CHAPTER 7 *Bristol-Blenheims...* 101

insufficient. The first Monocoupes which had arrived in Damascus, then, were shifted to Rayack, a base under the command of Major Denis [pronounce duh-NEE]. **Jacques Drabier** [pronounce drah-BYAY] was at this time assigned to the G.M.I., the Mixed Teaching and War Mission Group, of Damascus, where he had been stationed since March 19, 1942, having joined the Free French Air Force* in June of 1940 [sic] and having then undergone training with the Royal Air Force in England.

This is the interview:

"They turned me loose on those Monocoupes starting on March 9, 1943. I was under orders to put in a lot of hours so I could assume my post as instructor right away. These Monocoupes did more than serve as trainers for student pilots, since they performed rescue missions, plus carried documents in what we called *liaison* missions as well as regular mail. As recompense, the hardworking mechanics enjoyed a ride on a Monocoupe from time to time and this consolidated our team spirit. I had about fifty students during that time, some needing a refresher course, some needing to perfect their navigation skills and some needing to train for flights in tight formation. The Monocoupe was a good way, too, for pilots to get the hours they needed to obtain different licenses. This plane helped students feel safer in adverse conditions like crosswinds, forced landings or ultra-short landings. For all of that, the Monocoupe was the perfect tool."

* established 7 July 1940

Note the machinegun, which had a "stop" to prevent shooting the tail, on this Potez 25 used for desert surveillance.

War Pilot Memoirs: A Mirror on 1939

CHAPTER 8

My Head in a Basket
or
Narrow Escape ... like James Bond

On the twenty-second of October, 1943, a Friday, I flew to where General de Gaulle's pilot was broken down. I transported repair parts and the mechanic himself.

My flight log shows one hour five minutes Rayack – Gaza – Mistaff, then one hour Mistaff – Gaza (Palestine), then one hour fifteen minutes Gaza – Pétah Tiava [sic], which is properly Petah Tikva, a village near the city of Jaffa which is in modern-day Israel. To make it back to the base at Rayack it only took an hour and a half; this was the following day. No trouble was encountered. Since I knew the lay of the land better than the other pilots, they often called on me for these *dépannage* missions, whether for flat tires, lack of gasoline or more serious motor trouble.

That Monocoupe airplane always impressed me for its surprising capacity to swallow sand! Without a cough from the motor, you could even perform aerobatics, given a properly trained pilot at the controls. Capable of long distances in short time, she was not sensitive to sudden changes in the weather, and she could climb high when the need should arise.

One time I got sent to Baghdad to bring back some sacks of mail; in fact, the mail-sacks filled the plane to the ceiling. I had to check in with "relay" landing strips numbered "T1", etc., which were emergency landing strips with fuel tanks and a little shack or impromptu control tower. In order to "check in", we usually didn't talk over the radio but simply waved off with our wings as we passed over. Our planes had one bright landing headlight plus green lights on one side and red on the other, but these didn't flash. I do remember flashing lights from "relay" strips giving messages in Morse Code, though. When a guy needed to go pee-pee, these landing strips came in handy. Likewise, if a control cable seemed to have too much slack, you'd touch down, pull out your handy-dandy flashlight and crawl to the back of the fuselage, which was all of fifteen feet from propeller to tail.

On this particular mission there was no alternate route: it was necessary to hit ten thousand feet of altitude to shuffle over the plateau of Lake Tiberiade. This was nearly the maximum for a Monocoupe, and as I scooted my little butt over the top, I held my breath, at what seemed like the height of the fishing boat masts on the lake! Carburetors were persnickety and detested that very thin air. In my mind's ear I can still hear the "poof, poof... poof-poof-poof" of the motor, and I knew that losing just fifty rpm or so could dunk me into the lake. After that: whew! As a reward to myself, I made a detour to the seashore.

*   *   *

Unexpected Attack in Damascus

In the deep dark reaches of central Damascus, a little altercation took place, and I was involved. The whole region is Muslim, and you should picture this particular ghetto as quite poor. This part of town, though, boasted one of our favorite restaurants as well as our dojo for studying Judo. There were three of us, all from Picardie Squadron: Jean Godin, Jean Ducourneau and I. We mingled with the masses at this dojo, really just a little house set up for workouts.

There was a Navy man, a Red Belt (highest), who worked us out. The three of us were black belts and I myself had four white stripes on my shoulder indicating Tai-chi-chuan, Karate,

CHAPTER 8 *My Head in a Basket* 105

Nanchaku and Jiu-jitsu. One particular evening, after working out and realizing it was only seven o'clock, we sensed a nighttime freshness in the air which perked the appetite. Instead of heading back to the base we voted for couscous; this little restaurant had a purely Eastern menu. It was situated in a badly reputed and rundown part of town, yet this did not discount the fact that their cuisine was top notch. As with many buildings in that area, you had to mount a skinny staircase which had its steps formed out of large rocks embedded in the wall. There was no handrail, notwithstanding a good twenty or more steps to navigate, so a person not paying attention really could get hurt. Why no handrail? Well what do I know, but think of it as a Moorish stylistic quirk of architecture. Having navigated the steps, you reached a bigger landing just outside the door of the restaurant.

Once we'd finished our meal, out we came, boisterous as could be. Just as we were preparing to descend that infamous stairway, below us, halfway up, we saw three Arabs dressed in raggedy old clothes. They were coming our way, they had an underhanded demeanor, and they had three of those curved Arabian knives too! Quickly enough we deciphered their intentions, yet we were stuck between the proverbial rock and a hard place: no way to back out and too high up to jump. In a snap, our minds solidified as to one course of action. Whispering to each other... although later I realized there hadn't been any need since our opponents didn't speak French, a certain advantage to fighting at the international level... we called our shots. Since I was on the left, the wide open side, between gritted teeth I said I'd take the guy on the left. "Godin, take the middle. Ducourneau, the right." We stood our ground. Those coco heads, all perplexed, didn't know what was up. After a moment of hesitation, they started up the stairs toward us, brandishing their weapons in sweeping circles. We stayed put, waiting for the perfect moment.

About the time they got within an arm's length, I set to

screaming, very loudly, "Kee – EYE," our martial arts battle cry. In three distinct movements I managed to gain control of the guy in front of me, before clobbering him with eight or ten Karate blows. He lost his balance and fell off into the void, and from a height of a good twenty feet. He crash landed, semiconscious. As for the other two, I can remember their rolling down the stairway, giving out incoherent screams. Well, well… nothing moving. We descended cautiously. The two that had rolled down were the first on their feet, and I managed to put my fist once more into my guy, who was sluggish at best. Off they ran, as if heading for the hills… as if the Devil himself were after them.

After a quick look around, we congratulated each other with handshakes, laughing all the while. Off we walked to the barracks. It had been an unexpected battle, very impromptu, which demonstrated for us how martial arts training can be efficient, and how Judo and such are not always disciplines of luxury.

*   *   *

Whenever we went on weekend leave it meant two solid days of liberty, so we'd go to Damascus. My buddies knew a few French families they could pass the time with, relaxing and rehabilitating. As for me, I knew no one. I preferred sort of being alone, independent. I used to love walking around Damascus, an intriguing city, really, with its bright, multicolor storefronts, the monuments, and of course the famous Umayyad Mosque with its gold domes. Since we French were seen as infidels, we didn't have the right to enter, and for fear of having my throat slit I generally respected such rules.

Wisely, then, I found safe haven at the movies, and often. The Souks, those distinctively Arab dwellings usually situated above a retail operation, were in a sub-city of their own. The Souks were located within a very lofty protective wall. There were massive doorways with gates that got opened at sunrise and shut tight

CHAPTER 8 *My Head in a Basket*

at sunset, and you did not want to dilly dally too much, whether shopping or just whiling away the time. Unlike in some settings, unlike when you have a bell, say, that tolls for vespers, there was no audible reminder in the Souks. You would be genuinely cloistered for the night. Well, this event came my way.

*   *   *

To be as comfortable as possible on military leave, one very affordable place to rest was in a brothel. For a few francs, you could save yourself the trouble of traipsing around looking for a hotel. These gals pampered me. No worries: they were under the strictest sanitary monitoring, and they'd easily have rivaled the geishas of Japan.

One particular evening I had yet to decide where to spend the night, so I went in to see a Jean Gabin movie; he was the "Clark Gable" of France. I was alone, and it was really restful to be alone sometimes. I seated myself. The theater seat on my left was empty, but not for long. There arrived the most elegant dark-skinned beauty I've ever seen, veil across her face. Her garment was of semitransparent silk, and right through her veil you could perceive the prettiest face. Her pitch black hair was held in place by diamond-encrusted barrettes. She seated herself close to me as she sized me up, all the while holding ever so delicately the lower portion of her veil, that very typical, feminine gesture. Her eyes alone were fully visible, and wow were they striking: long black lashes, and eyelids delicately tinted with a dark shade that accentuated her deep gaze.

The movie began. The lights went down. I noticed my attractive neighbor had removed her veil and with the light from the movie screen I could perceive a face both refined and enticing. Now, of course, it was my turn to face her way and admire her, to size her up. She picked up on this and faced me square on. Our eyes met, and she smiled at me.

A bit later I felt a delicate hand being poised upon my own. My hand was simply limp upon the armrest. Oo-la-la, what a sensation. She smiled, but without moving. Such an event as this seemed very abnormal: here sat an aristocratic lady of Arabian origin flirting with me. Surely these women, generally shut off from the world, would not typically dare such a maneuver. They were seen escorted by armed guards, and not only for protection but for having their conduct monitored. Surely bad conduct got reported back to the man of the house!

Finding these palpitating events to be quite pleasant, I was happy that we then engaged in quite a long conversation, at whispering level. Many a time she smiled at me; I vividly recall her gorgeous white teeth. Her French was impeccable. Her name was Djedina, and when I told her my name and that I flew for the Free French Air Force, she said she wanted to get to know me better, being a big fan of aviators. Hmm. Yes, I decided. I was indeed surprised at her candor. When I asked if she was alone, she didn't voice a reply but rather shook her head as she pointed to the seat behind me. It contained her bodyguard, complete with handlebar moustache and, alas, a big knife on his belt. When I turned to get a look at him, he simply smiled. Ok. He seems to be going along. Still whispering, Djedina said, "He's faithful to me. He'll do whatever I ask of him. You can put your trust in him."

Then Djedina set herself to plotting out the evening's program. She said, "I'll walk out alone when the movie's over. Don't follow me immediately, but when you do come out my bodyguard will point you to my limousine. If you wish, you'll get in. This way we'll be away from public view." She continuously smiled at me and thus I could not resist. I signaled yes by nodding my head. Once more I took a look at that bone-crushing bronze statue of a bodyguard. The whole situation seemed surreal, and I couldn't get over it. This lady presented neither the impression of a prostitute nor that of a person prone to misconduct,

CHAPTER 8 *My Head in a Basket*

and certainly not the mundane appearance of women we were accustomed to seeing around us in the streets of Damascus. By this time, I really was perplexed. Nonetheless, I decided to follow her instructions to the letter.

After the movie I found myself in her limousine. Wow, Djedina was a beauty. Her veil completely removed, her bodice halfway exposed, I was flying with the angels. She took both my hands into her lap and told the driver to go. Where were we headed? I had no clue. All I knew was that I was in the presence of a gorgeous woman who kept speaking to me in the most heavenly voice, saying, "Don't worry. All my servants are faithful to me. My husband is away in Jordan for four days. We'll be able to relax undistracted."

Now this revelation made me lose my breath a bit. Married, huh? I knew well the moral rules, the customs of these Muslims and suddenly I could see my own head cut off and tossed aside in a ditch somewhere! Now I came to understand why "don't worry" was her favorite phrase. By the events that were to follow I learned that bodyguards were often in on this kind of clandestine rendezvous. These women were both sheltered and deprived of sexual gratification, in contrast to their husbands who had frequent business trips, etcetera. This was just for starters, since many husbands had harems to drain them dry. My mind was made up, yet only via a whirlwind of emotions. All my senses were steering me to the one logical bounty: to hold this gorgeous female in my arms, to get a taste of Arabian delight.

Djedina explained that she couldn't take me to her own home, but that we were going to a property belonging to a good friend whose home was also inside the walls I described around the Souks. The friend was a reputable merchant who was fully aware of Djedina's freelance pleasures. I began to trust that she and her friend really did keep secrets.

This dwelling, elegant and luxurious, was unimposing as you

approached. What was this night like for me? Be it known that human hands cannot write such ecstasy. Imagine if you will, transparent India muslin all around. Imagine, too, a perfumed fountain which is gurgling, and all of it set to the softest music coming out of nowhere. Imagine if you will, a real life version of Aladdin from <u>The Arabian Nights</u>, and Aladdin was I.

The time was about two o'clock a.m. when suddenly strong taps on the door awakened us. She covered up as she slid out of bed, then went to the door which she opened part way. What was happening? I knew nothing; she spoke in Arabic. She shut the door again, then, with a troubled way about her, yet with the continued blinking of those big gorgeous eyes of hers, she said, "Get dressed quickly. They say my husband is back early. He must have changed his plans." According to the guards, he was about a half an hour away which would give me plenty of time. I would be able to get out safely, but I was to remain alert! She entrusted my safe passage to one of her guards who would get me to a secret doorway out of the Souks. This doorway was a passage through the big wall. As for Djedina, she'd be taking off posthaste to her own place.

Needless to say my mood was one of panic and my throat was seizing upon itself. I was really seeing my head in a basket now. As an oddity in the architecture of the Souks, one house seemed to hug right up to the next, as if they were one solid block. My noble guide seemed to take us up, up, up, then down, down, down incessantly. At times we'd go through tunnels then find ourselves up on a flat roof again. Finally, after a half hour of being guided through this labyrinth, I found myself standing before a gate that surely would not be unlocked until dawn.

As I hope I have succeeded in communicating, dear Reader, I was not at all at ease. My infamous big friend, the devil with the horned moustache, led me toward a smaller gateway only barely visible. At this gateway stood a guard. They exchanged a few

CHAPTER 8 *My Head in a Basket*

lines of Arabic gibberish. I was the happiest man on Earth when the one opened up the door, giving me a sign. Oh, he did not fail to hold out his cupped hand, of course. I quickly enough understood, and I was only too happy to tip him well. My thanks go to Allah for having had enough money in my pocket to make it happen.

Never again did I see Djedina. I bet she found another lover and I bet he was from the French Foreign Legion. Thinking it through as I reread now, once in your life you have to be young and stupid enough to engage in such. Boldness mixed with the seeking of prestige can yield some crazy results. No matter what, though, I live on without regret. I don't believe I'd do it again, but what a memorable and delicious night! My escapade within the walls of the Souks let me know a woman of extreme beauty.

War Pilot Memoirs: A Mirror on 1939

CHAPTER 9

Swimming Pool Romance

Lieutenant Colonel Morlaix had been key in setting up the F.A.F.L., the Free French Air Force, in England during June of 1940. Note that "Morlaix" was his wartime pseudonym, a trick that helped maintain anonymity for your family back home, helped keep the Germans from punishing your family for your being a soldier. He had flown with two squadrons of the Royal Air Force, racking up twenty-three kills. He was in charge of our aviation there in Syria and Lebanon from January of 1943 right through 1944.

By my flight log, my final flight in a Monocoupe was 01 November, 1943, and around that time I had the privilege of having a drink with Lieutenant Colonel Morlaix. He was on his way to England. He shared with me that he agreed this decision to send me along with the group to Syria had been a dirty trick. He was sympathetic that I could have been just as easily stationed with the RAF in England. It's true that I was one of the few flight instructors at Rayack wearing RAF wings.

In late 1943, Flight Sergeants Ducourneau, Scalone and Siven became monitors for the Monocoupe. At my request, then, H.Q. in Beirut reassigned me to flying various other models. I was soon to pilot Hurricanes equipped with "feltas" which were special sand filters for the airflow. The war effort was calling more and more upon the Hurricane for advanced types of missions, but in preparation for this I had to fly the Harvard T-6, a trainer which could rapidly be fitted with a machinegun and zoom off to the Syrian, Turkish or Iranian border. The *Groupe Ardennes* was named for that mountainous region of France where the Battle of the Bulge would soon occur, and its Commanding Officer was Captain Max Vinçotte [pronounce vîn-SUHHT, -în rhyming with Chopin]. In order to perfect my aerobatics and fly in tight formation and pilot blindly, it was required that I put in many hours on the Morane Saulnier. Among the very first, I had just been assigned to the *Groupe Ardennes*, and this led to my being accepted to pilot the Hurricane.

This well-reputed British aircraft had come off the production lines before the Spitfire, and the *Groupe Ardennes* had just received several of them. My yearning to fly this Hurricane Challenger II almost got realized in December of 1943, but alas they kept me on Moranes and on Stamps because of the great need for escort missions of convoys on the ground. It was the Stamp that we knew for upside-down flying, and the reader should know how uneasy we pilots were about flying upside down. You see, when the plane was inverted, so were the directions in which you had to push or pull the controls. For example, you pull on the stick to climb in normal conditions, but when upside-down one had to push! It was not at all an easy reversal of commands to grow accustomed to, yet it was a crucial one. Some pilots, faced with cases where an unexpected burst of wind flipped the plane over, died, since the first and natural reaction was to pull on the stick. God, no! This was exactly the command to send a plane down to impact the soil. A perilous joker in the deck of cards, this maneuver could be a trump card also. A pilot accustomed to flying on his back could surprise the enemy and take him down.

CHAPTER 9 *Swimming Pool Romance*

Casba Tadla, Morocco: Hell

May, 1944. Things were shaking up. The Americans had opened a training base in northwest Africa, at Casba Tadla, Morocco, and the airplane model "Hurricane" was losing its popularity as it got replaced by others. Instead of sending me back to England to be incorporated into the RAF or the *Groupe Alsace*, my superiors ushered me off to Morocco to do some more Harvard T-6. On June 1st, 1944, I was up in three planes: for thirty-five minutes I flew a Harvard as student pilot on dual controls, then as copilot on the Dauntless numbered DA24745 we took forty minutes outbound, and finally for an hour and forty minutes inbound I was the pilot of a Morane. All of these maneuvers were under four thousand feet, and the first was under two thousand.

My 22nd birthday was June 3rd, 1944, and I got invited to the bar there at the mess for a glass of champagne. I remember thinking what a nice gesture it was on the part of my buddies. Just a few days later I was sent up in a Curtis P-36, a faster plane, and I flew a mock-combat as an exercise. The time had come for me seriously to grasp what dive-bombing was all about, and we possessed really good planes: Dauntless A-24s, with their perforated, oversized wing flaps which were designed to slow us down. These Dauntless A-24s had recently arrived from the U.S. Navy where newer planes had fold-up wings. Considerably reducing the airspeed in a dive, these perforated wing flaps gave us time to manipulate the more accurate release of our bombs.

There was a mandatory exercise: attempting to land in "short space", that is to say upon a limited runway such as what you'd find on an aircraft carrier. They had us make attempts on our own runways, with aircraft carrier dimensions marked in white chalk as a simulation. Not even once did I succeed at making a proper landing. Always overshooting, if there had been a real aircraft carrier I'd have been "in the drink" right along with the machine! This just wasn't my strong suit.

We alternated between the Curtis and the Morane for upside-down training. This was real upside-down flying; we had no simulators. Our superior officers wanted us to be comfortable on several models. This airbase called Casba Tadla, near Meknès [pronounce meck-NEZZ], Morocco, became the school for fighter-bombers. Using A-24s, we practiced firing on targets from a low altitude, releasing bombs on old worn-out tanks or trucks, or simulated antiaircraft batteries. Descending from twenty thousand feet, the pilot would see his target looking no bigger than a dime. It was surprising how rapidly this "coin" became the size of a dinner plate, and this seemed to happen all of a sudden. It was at this moment you had to release your bombs and climb. A little hesitation could cause impact with Mother Earth. The training then progressed to moving targets, namely one rickety old car being towed by another. There were only a few dozen yards of distance between cars, so I was glad to be in the sky and not driving the lead car! You embrace the scenario.

Meknès: Sentimental Adventure

With temperatures over 100°F and high humidity, this training camp near the town of Casba Tadla, Morocco, was a living Hell. With such high temperatures, the thin air of the afternoon did not support flight operations. Flying at that time of day could be dangerous, especially in our heavier models like the Curtis P-36 and the A-24 Dauntless. So, then, we often got leave to go into the city.

Meknès was a lovely urban setting, and one particular day I was walking with some buddies toward the municipal swimming pool. To call a dip in the pool "refreshing" would be a vast understatement, since the heat was at its typical level like brimstone. We were disappointed to find this swimming pool crowded to overflowing; of course, locals and military alike all had the same idea. I had noticed, just a hundred yards away, some other swimming pools surrounded by thick hedges and flowering plants and

CHAPTER 9   *Swimming Pool Romance*   117

encircled by little walls which supported steel grids on top. Surely, these had to be private pools.

We walked over to read the signs, which verified it was a *cercle sportif*, an athletic club for members only. Prim and proper, we turned around to head back to that overflowing madhouse, to that "ant farm" of a public pool. Just then two young girls came walking up, both brunette, both very pretty. They caught our eye, of course, as the two of them headed for a gateway in the fence. With the highest moral standards and only the best of honest intentions based upon curiosity, we went over to find out who owned this complex. They smiled at us, looking very amused, as they looked us over from head to toe. Politely they informed us of what we already knew: these were private pools. Oh, well. They whispered back and forth to each other, and after a slight pause one of them said, "Messieurs, these pools are private but we have the right to invite you in. What would you say to that?"

We overflowed with joy, so it was with a forced little controlled smile that I answered, "Now that would be very kind of you." No sooner said than done: we followed them.

Doing the introductions, one brunette said, "My name is Meelou, for Melanie." The other, who was more forward, more candid, presented herself as Tanya. She looked to be of Slavic origin and was very cute. We all entered this complex where the grounds were quaint and the pools were exquisite.

I learned that Meelou's dad was Director for the railway network of the north coast of Morocco, and that her older brother was serving in the French Navy, though it was the *Marine de Vichy*, that unwelcome government of southern France. I thought "Meelou" was a cute nickname. She was 19 years old and about my size. She wore her hair down since it was lovely and full, covering her shoulders. The pool was huge yet mostly empty, both girls were good swimmers and they enjoyed surprising us guys via underwater attack from time to time. We boys, in turn, acted out a bit, and I think for Meelou and Tanya it was a grand

and unexpected adventure. The girls told us how all their friends were off serving in the military and how lonely it was there in Meknès. I sympathized in particular with Meelou, who seemed to be such a lonely heart. For the time being I must have been a comfort to her, and for me, I'll admit, the whole scenario was an unexpected pleasure.

That evening, Meelou and I parted with a promise to see each other a week later. Our *au revoir* was filled with promises, and there was passionate kissing. She insisted that I visit her home, which turned out to be in a nice middleclass neighborhood, to meet her mother and her sister. She showed me the school she was attending. We got together way too often, way too fast; one says *trop vite* [pronounce troh veet] in French. Deep feelings of attachment developed on her side and she declared herself to be in love with me, and she was even making future plans. Sadly I had to reveal to her the fact I was engaged to a lovely Englishwoman who awaited me in Great Britain. Meelou stared at me with eyes all full of tears as she started sobbing, and I was both ashamed and troubled. I must admit that I felt for her too; oh, boy, what a predicament.

I tried rationalizing with Meelou, but the harder I tried the more she latched onto me. Still crying, she said, "Do you love her more than me, your Englishwoman?" In vain attempts, I elaborated on how this was different.

This went on for a month. There was no reasoning with Meelou; all my little attempts to wiggle out of this failed. I began, at least, to understand her, this gentle creature, so loving, intelligent and charming... yet stuck on the idea of marrying me! Her mother had become aware of Meelou's love for me but not of the fact that I had a fiancée elsewhere, so Mother was staying out of it, to let things run their course. It was imperative that I find a way to resolve all this. But what to do?

Since my training was coming to an end, it would surely be any day now that I'd get shipped off to some squadron. Meelou's distress caused me a great deal of anguish, so I was glad when

CHAPTER 9 *Swimming Pool Romance*

her mother invited me for a meal with the supplemental invitation to come a bit early, before Meelou's arrival, so Mother and I could discuss the situation. She shared with me that Meelou had attempted suicide. Whoa! I deemed myself the guilty party for her daughter's state of mind.

There was a girlfriend who had brought Meelou home from a somber scene. She had found Meelou seated in the middle of the railroad tracks, and quite a way from the station. She recounted how Meelou's reply had been "I don't want to live anymore," when the girlfriend had asked what in the world she was doing.

My God! I comforted the mother by saying that I simply had to do something before something dreadful might occur. Providence was on our side, since the Base Commander had indeed received orders for me to be dispatched. I was to leave the very next day and be attached to *Groupe 3/6 Roussillon*, a fighter squadron stationed at Algeria's capital city, at a base called *Maison Blanche*.

I explained to Meelou's mother that we war pilots flew plenty of sorties and that any one of them could prove to be our last, whether by being wounded or just not coming back at all. Being shot down, well, it was just a possible outcome we had to live with. Anyway, for the purpose of bringing Meelou's distress to an end, I promised to arrange that a telegram be sent reporting me as lost in action. I would seek the complicity of my Commanding Officer, and I would wait just two weeks after leaving Morocco.

So, Meelou's mother and I reached an accord. The telegram was indeed sent, it bore the official squadron coding, and it conveyed the customary condolences. I had, to this end, explained to my superior how acute the situation really was, and he had shown great compassion for the anguish of our circumstances. Feeling discouraged, I admitted to myself how shamefully I'd behaved, but this way Meelou could be sorrowful justifiably. Furthermore she would not have to sense acute rejection. Know, dear Reader, that all of this had affected me gravely also. I felt remorse, and I made myself the solemn promise never again to toy with destiny, and certainly not to toy with the heart of a precious young girl. I had no further contact, I've had no further news and I never learned the precise outcome there in Meknès; it's better this way. Just the memory of it all, even today, can bring tears to my eyes. I really must confess right here: I loved her very much.

Jacques and Meelou

War Pilot Memoirs: A Mirror on 1939

CHAPTER 10

The Flying Snake

On the tarmac at Meknès the Americans had three or four Hurricanes. We got instruction on these and other planes about how to fly to get behind your opponent; you had to be on an opponent's tail to bring him down. We performed circling combat exercises, also called dogfights.

On October 3rd, 1944, I was ordered to go up in Hurricane #410 and another pilot boarded a second one. The takeoffs were spaced fifteen minutes apart. There I was at thirty thousand feet ready to undertake my simulated twist-and-turn combat. Unexpectedly a third fighter and pilot showed up, but he was acting rather nonchalant, there only to roll film. I got congratulated after landing, twice the victor based on documented cinematic evidence.

It was a pinnacle to my enthusiasm when I got told I was good to go: ready to fly the combat missions which were forthcoming. Our squadron leader, Blanek, gave me a boost of morale in telling me I'd be up the very next day in a P-39 Airacobra. We had only just gotten them, but they'd had the once-over from our mechanics, so they were ready to fire up and take off.

October, 1944. In a few weeks of time several Bell P-39 Airacobras (Air Cobras) had been delivered. The ground crewmen had done their inspections, readying them for the flight instructors. On this model there was no provision for dual controls, so a student pilot had to be pretty focused, given all the new instruments plus an auxiliary fuel tank. Focusing on bomb release mechanisms was particularly important. There was a cannon, and the diameter of its barrel was 37mm which is an inch and a half. Such a thing was altogether new to us.

Up until this time all the planes we'd flown had possessed the standard little wheel at the back end. While taxiing, one had to avoid obstacles on the ground. Pilots were forced to look out of the cockpit from left to right because the motor, rising before us at an incline, blocked our view. The Airacobra was a horizontal apparatus since the nose wheel made any tail wheel unnecessary, so the reader can visualize why we called it "the tricycle." Up in the tricycle cockpit you could look straight forward to see out and this really helped us at takeoff. Your peripheral vision functioned for what was going on alongside and you could see forward at the same time. A unique quirk had the motor located behind the pilot. This was something we pilots, all of us males, talked about, since we had to straddle the turning machinery which might have threatened certain anatomical parts!

This plane had gained widespread use after the attack on Pearl Harbor three years earlier. Like most fighter-bombers, it was engineered to be flown to the target, then release bombs and/or any fuel tanks, and finally perform strafing on the ground. With bombs or tanks attached, you certainly didn't want to engage in aerial combat. Imagine, for me, what a contrast to my pal Tauzi, machinegun on a turret, in the back end of an open-cockpit Potez! We especially appreciated the Airacobra's cannon up there dead center of the prop. Our Airacobra motors had no superchargers, which actually helped us handle them at lower altitudes.

Bell produced nine and a half thousand Airacobras, of which about half went to the British, the Russians, and our Free French Forces. The reader mustn't fail to recognize the high performance these planes were capable of: top speed of over 350 mph, ceiling of 35,000 feet and range of 650 miles. Its Allison V-1710 touted twelve hundred horsepower. In addition to that infamous 37mm cannon, you found two .50-caliber (half-inch diameter) machineguns in the nose plus two more under-wing, not to forget a bomb of either five hundred or one thousand pounds under the belly.

What a magnificent piece of work, and we really did some damage with this *oiseau* (bird), but we mustn't forget her problematic idiosyncrasies. She was risky to fly, especially when she'd spin out. Furthermore, dropping just fifty or so rpm could mess you up, causing the plane to lose lift. She was tough to handle at slow speeds. Let me elaborate.

The American fly-boys despised the Airacobra, calling it the "flying iron." They were comparing its heavy handling to a clothes iron. Later on I found out the actual planes they sent us had been declared out of service. How did they manage to pass off these dangerous machines on us? The Americans didn't want to lose their pilots, but surely we had a right to value our skins too.

There had been no particular model of plane designated for us of the F.A.F.L., so we went lamenting at the doorstep of the Allies. When our Headquarters found out that these P-39s were being discarded by order of General Eisenhower, our people consulted with his people. "What's the difference, gentlemen, if you send your machines our way, to our pilots who have no other resources, who can make use of them notwithstanding the problems." Better than nothing, precise warnings to pilots would have to suffice. And that was that.

Ike was convinced that we deserved better. He sent word that we should be patient. He had something in store for us which would be a full ten times superior to these P-39s. He was alluding to the infamous Republic P-47 Thunderbolt! Every guy at the base was overwhelmed with joy.

In the meantime, I got a kick out of how this P-39 handled on takeoff. Smoothly and quickly it left the ground thanks to that horizontal angle. You had to come in at high speed for a landing, though. On one occasion I failed twice at landing, having to abort each time, nervously heading for the sky again. On my third approach, even with groundspeed a bit above normal which makes your plane roll too fast, I managed to brake hard and stop. You always had to bear in mind the risk of a blowout, just as on the freeway. One other time, having the same difficulty landing, I really thought I was going to "swallow" the barracks at the end of the runway.

Alas, after about twenty flight hours, I started to know the quirks of this "Cobra." Well known as a plane that could bite you, we all paid close attention to what we were doing.

That cannon really was a godsend. In training, I recall piercing an old dilapidated army tank with an Airacobra cannon, and the projectile went through it like a hot knife through butter. A curious recommendation came from my monitor, putting me on the alert: "Don't ever fire twice on the same target with that cannon. You'll bite the dust." Apparently this mistake would cut the airspeed suddenly and send the plane into the ground without warning. Hmm... worth remembering.

P-39 Airacobra,
year 1944

Grandfather

Grandmother

My mother, Pauline

My father, René

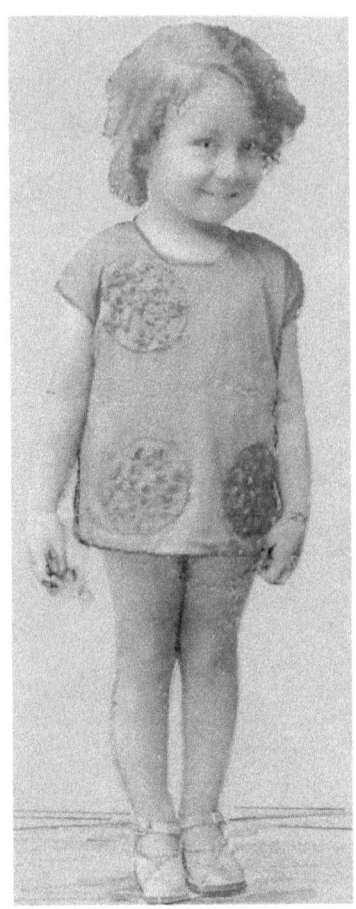

Me, "Jackie", at age 2½.

My father & I

Flood caused by torrential rain

Mekong River, *habitation flottante*: floating village

My first communion

Age 15, Beaux Arts School, in Paris

Engineering school: it got cold in Paris

My English flat metallic bow

"Curare" tree, sap used to poison arrows

Young Moï girls

Strolling merchants, Saigon

Moï merchant

Me, in a *pousse-pousse*, a rickshaw

Aunt Betty, on their plantation, with two baby tigers

Boulok and his Moï keeper

Me, with Moï safari guides

Boulok as a cub

My sketch of a strolling merchant

How I recall that crocodile hunting by the natives

Stukas attack the Red Cross train

Sergeant J.P. Drabier

René Moine

The skipper of the Trébouliste, Captain François Lelguen

On the deck of the Trébouliste (1940) escaping to England

Luciole Caudron, a trainer

Tiger Moth, a British trainer

De Gaulle & Churchill (left), allies & friends

Hitler, Germany's Chancellor.

A TOUS LES FRANÇAIS

La France a perdu une bataille!
Mais la France n'a pas perdu la guerre!

Des gouvernants de rencontre ont pu capituler, cédant à la panique, oubliant l'honneur, livrant le pays a la servitude. Cependant, rien n'est perdu!

Rien n'est perdu, parce que cette guerre est une guerre mondiale. Dans l'univers libre, des forces immenses n'ont pas encore donne. Un jour, ces forces ecraseront l'ennemi. Il faut que la France, ce jour-là, soit presente à la victoire. Alors, elle retrouvera sa liberte et sa grandeur. Tel est mon but, mon seul but!

Voila pourquoi je convie tous les Francais, ou qu'ils se trouvent, à s'unir a moi dans l'action, dans le sacrifice et dans l'esperance.

Notre patrie est en peril de mort.
Luttons tous pour la sauver!

VIVE LA FRANCE !

Tours, France
Year 1940

Private Drabier
2 months after enlisting

Badge of the
student pilot: his first "wing"

St. Athan, England 7/7/1940
I am in the middle.

Luciole Caudron

Training at a school near Dinard: a Cri-Cri

Student pilots, Morlaix School #23, waiting to fly (monitored) using dual controls

Harvard AT-5

Miles Master training, R.A.F.

Ha! "First class" travel between Algiers and Casablanca

Camberley, England, where they teach us to march

Lebanon

A nurse in Lebanon (me on the right)

Monitor/Instructors in Damascus
Left to right: unknown, me, Anselme, Monguillot, Fauvel

Damascus, Syria (I am the third from the right, with a cap)

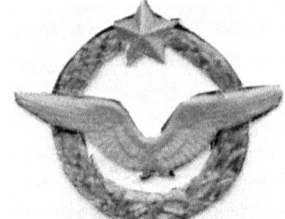

French Pilot Insignia

Sergent-chef Gollay strikes a concrete mile-marker in a Potez 25

Crew of Blenheim IV, left to right:
Radio Sergeant Hamer,
Sergent-chef Maurice Vergès,
Unknown mechanic,
Sergent-chef Jacques Drabier (me),
Sergent-chef Jean Ducourneau

Bell Airacobra P-39

Tomahawk P-40

Dauntless A-24, dive bomber training

Sergent-chef Drabier (me), instructor for Monocoupe-Franklin 90AF, Damascus 1942

Sgt./J. Drabier

Above the plane
Cdt. Noël

Cne. Guigonis
Co. of gc. Picardie.
Damas (Syria-1942)

Adjt./ Ballator
Chief instructor

Damascus 1942

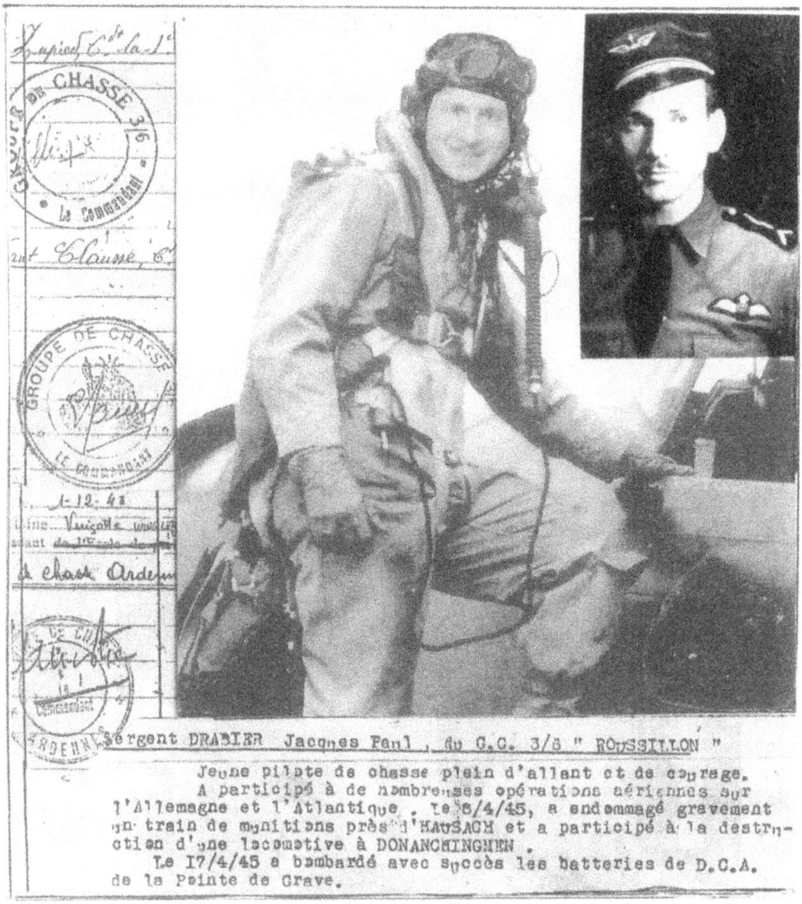

Sergent DRABIER Jacques Paul , du G.C. 3/6 " ROUSSILLON "

Jeune pilote de chasse plein d'allant et de courage.
A participé à de nombreuses opérations aériennes sur l'Allemagne et l'Atlantique . Le 8/4/45, a endommagé gravement un train de munitions près d'HAUSACH et a participé à la destruction d'une locomotive à DONANCHINGNEN .
Le I7/4/45 a bombardé avec succès les batteries de D.C.A. de la Pointe de Grave.

High altitude mission, 30 pounds of equipment: Drabier in his P-47, the mighty "jug"

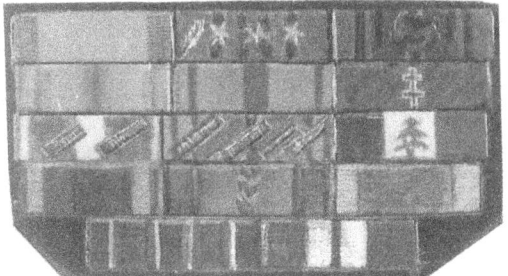

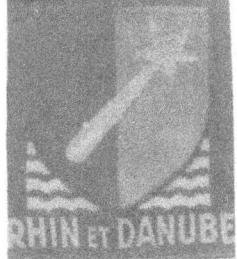

My WWII decoration & Medals (from left to right)
• Medaille Militaire-Croix de guerre avec Palme et "etoiles d'or
• Croix de la resistance • Médaille de combatant volunteer
• Médaille des F.A.F.L. • Extrême Orient (Syria)
• (Méditerranée-Italie- Allemagne) • Médaille de la Victoire
• Mérite Libanais • Commemorative Yugoslavia 41-45

Patch at top of left sleeve: German operations

Battle of the Bulge (Bastogne) 1944

Cordon of Merit for
the Battle of the Bulge

I am wearing the Cordon of Merit,
for having destroyed, 23 DEC 1944,
some "Tiger Tanks"

P-47 with my 500 pounds bomb

Night flight

Squadron called "3/6 Roussillon"; I am at the bottom right.

Loading bombs onto my P-47 at Luxeuil

My mechanic, Sgt. Boinot, harnessing me into the cockpit.
The P-47 had four mighty .50 caliber machineguns on EACH wing.

General Baudet pins the
médaille militaire on me.

Return from a mission in Germany (1945)

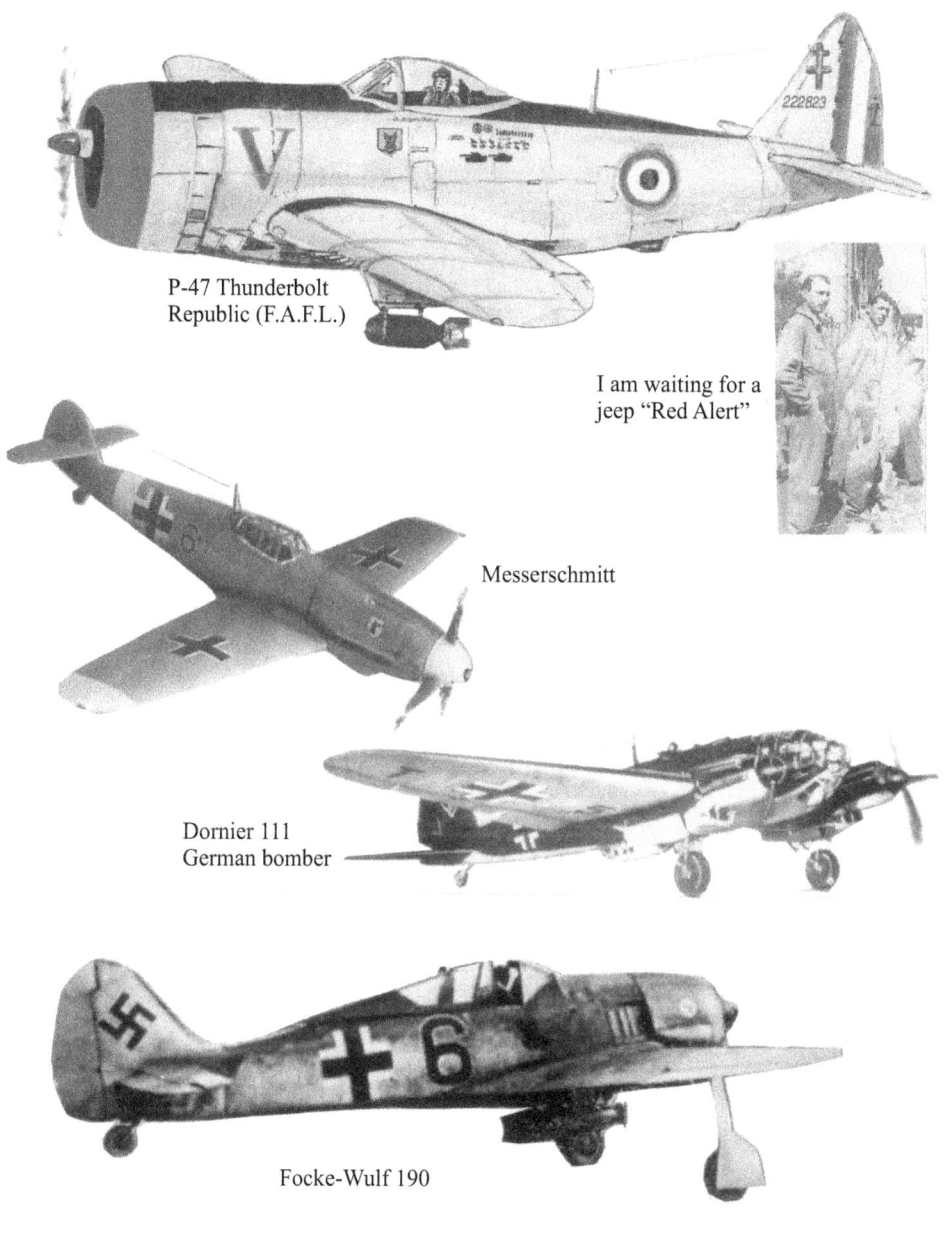

P-47 Thunderbolt
Republic (F.A.F.L.)

I am waiting for a jeep "Red Alert"

Messerschmitt

Dornier 111
German bomber

Focke-Wulf 190

De Gaulle reviews the troops.
Le Vallon, officers' mess.

Tauzi (left, me on right) my photographer and machine-gunner
aboard the Potez 25, Damascus

Rayack, Lebanon
Left to right: Sergeants Drabier, Gilles, Priest, Fournier
We monitors await the student pilots.

Umayyad Mosque, Damascus.
Tauzi took this actual photo from our Potez 25 at 600 feet.

Damascus 24 MAY 1942 Royal visit: Duke of Gloucester (shaking hands), on his right is General Catroux, on his left is Colonel Derry. General Valin (face partially hidden) is behind the Duke.

Natural gas reservoir near Royan, beside Aunt Lucie's house

Aunt Lucie Richard

Portrait: Joseph Weber, orchestra conductor of the Algiers Opera in Algeria

Joseph Weber and his wife, my cousin Jeanette

Just Married

Viane and *Maman* getting along very well together

Happy reunion with Tino, my guardian from before the war

My parent's house, built in 1885

Menotte, me and Tino

Aunt Betty Nant, underground freedom-fighter

My parents' house at Angoulins-sur-mer in Charente Maritime: my mother, Viane, my father

January, 1954, Dien Bien Phu (Vietnam)
My friend André Voirin on his Sikorsky H-19

Janine and André at his home,
village of Haulmé, in the Ardennes, France

André and I drinking to our WWII memories

Jacques Paul Drabier
Studied at Beaux Arts, Paris, and Engineering School Breguet, Paris.
Fighter pilot 1940-1945 for the Free French and the Royal Air Force.
Licensed: Civil Pilot for small crafts, Doctorate in Parapsychology.
Now retired in Goodyear, Arizona, USA.
Writer, speaker on UFOLOGY, television interviewee.

Janine, with John Hodges and his 1929 automobile.
This 2009 photo was taken in front of the Drabier home in Goodyear, Arizona.
John, also known as J. Anomdeplume, came to visit us as we compiled this book.
He lives in nearby Glendale with his wife Linda.

War Pilot Memoirs: A Mirror on 1939

CHAPTER 11

A Live Bomb for a Hockey Puck

The order had been given for us to join forces with Fighter Group 3/6 "Roussillon", so off we went from Morocco, the extreme northwest corner of Africa which descends to the Strait of Gibraltar, flying due east in our P-39s. We were headed for a temporary base in the Algiers suburb called Maison Blanche, today called Dar El Beïda. Both names translate as "White House" and it's the site of a major airport now as it was then. Algeria was still officially part of France. This stationing at Algiers would be temporary for a week or so, awaiting orders to head for our new airbase in Provence, the southeast corner of France. It was 1944 in the month of November. We were plenty impatient to get to Provence, but personally I was ecstatic to be in the city of Algiers since I would have a rare opportunity to visit my cousin.

My cousin Joseph Weber was really a cousin-in-law, being the husband of my first cousin Jeannette. I lodged at their house which was about two miles from Maison Blanche. He was a composer, and he was Chief Conductor of the Algiers Opera. It had been many years since I'd seen him and it was a real pleasure to get together: I, the music-lover, felt blessed to get to go to rehearsal. He used to say to me, "Jacquot, it's a shame your parents didn't push you into this field, 'cause you've got Music in your veins." Hmm. He was surely right, since even nowadays, at age 85-plus, I work at the piano without knowing how to read even a note, and I find myself playing Jazz, plus some popular tunes from memory, all to the great surprise of my wife to whom the piano truly belongs.

That day when I visited Cousin Joe, he said to me, "Let's go to rehearsal today. After that, I look forward to spending some time with you." I was happy as a lark and tremendously proud to be invited. After sharing a nice meal we took off in his Citroën, arriving soon enough in front of the Opera House. I helped out by grabbing his attaché-case as I got out of the car and steered myself toward the entrance.

I was walking in front, as Cousin Joe followed with his cello in its case, when he said, "Go on ahead. I forgot something." It must have been in the car which was parked across the street, so I kept walking. Suddenly a screech, a piercing screech, reached my ears. It was squealing tires! Bystanders cried out in dismay, my heart skipped a beat and I stopped in my tracks with a bad premonition. Oh, my God... I scurried, and I found out my cousin had been hit by a truck driven by a "Bedouin." There lay my cousin on the ground with no sign of life! After what seemed like forever, amidst all the hubbub there arrived an ambulance to take him to the hospital. I contacted his wife, my cousin, and she got to the Emergency Room right away. The doctor told her that he had suffered a skull fracture. He had died in the ambulance nearing the hospital. There had been no chance of survival, given the severity of his injuries.

It was hard for me to grasp what had just happened. I consoled my cousin Jeannette as best I could, but with such a catastrophe what could I really do? Just to make matters worse my orders came through for the city of Salon, in Provence, the South of France, and I was to leave within a few days. I was perturbed not only by the accident but also by having to leave Cousin Jeannette alone in grief and distress.

*   *   *

CHAPTER 11 *A Live Bomb for a Hockey Puck*

Our new base was at Salon-de-Provence near Marseille. The 16th of November, 1944, a Thursday. This was my first over-the-water flight in a P-39 Airacobra.

Back in France: Fighter-bomber P-47 Thunderbolt

Our training was plenty rigorous: every day saw us aboard a P-39. We needed to perfect our flying in tight formation, to do low-altitude fly-by operations in addition to maneuvering at high altitude in preparation for combat. All these exercises were important not only for efficiency but likewise crucial for the survival of everybody in the group. Above all you had to remember the constraints of a P-39 as you flew against an enemy airplane. She was touchy enough to send you crashing to the Earth if you lost speed at low altitude. Woe is you if you fire twice on the same target on the ground! There would be an antiaircraft gun focused on you if you did.

Early December, 1944: we were getting set for missions into Italy. The Luftwaffe was generally superior to us during this war, better equipped with their Messerschmitts, their Focke-Wulf 190s, Dorniers, Heinkel 111 bombers and their Fw 200 Condors. On the ground they had an army with well-trained troops and those almighty tanks. Moreover they had their navy with its infamous U-boat submarines. Our first missions involved spotting these U-boats and sinking them, but our vastly inadequate 500-pound bombs didn't do much. We should have had torpedoes, but on our P-39s there were none.

We got sent out to do ranging: determining distances for shots fired by allied battleships off the coast of Italy. I had the honor of directing fire for the *S.S. Georges Leygues*, an anti-submarine frigate with big guns on deck. The mission of this Free French Naval Forces' ship was to bombard San Remo. We flew over San Remo to perform ranging for long-distance shelling coming from the *Georges Leygues*. "Too short, too long?" Yet at the same time we had to swerve to avoid antiaircraft fire which the Italians were sending our way.

In the meantime they brought us good news: the infamous P-47 Thunderbolts were on their way to us. What a step-up in efficiency, in effectiveness on the enemy! These planes had incredible power, letting us strike deeper behind enemy lines, letting us attack with greater precision. The firepower was head and shoulders above what we'd had before: eight barrels at .50 caliber (half-inch) which spat almost eighty rounds per second combined. Flying to the farthest German landing strips, raining havoc upon planes on the ground, their hangars, their runways... all this was made possible by a fuel reservoir mounted under the fuselage. The Germans didn't anticipate this P-47 Republic, and it's my firm belief that this was the first time they started to **fear** us.

The order had now come for us to join the *Groupe de Chasse* (literally "Hunters' Group"), Fighter Group number 3/6, called "Roussillon." Major Clausse was in charge of both squadrons. It had been in September of 1944 when he'd arrived at the city of Salon-de-Provence, equipped with a P-39 Airacobra. Later he'd set up housekeeping near the hamlet of Vallon, outside of Saint-Rémy de Provence, with an improvised landing strip. There was an old chateau there which got converted into a Headquarters and an Officers' Mess.

Our missions were comprised of bombing and machinegun "strafing" raids on northern Italy. This campaign of 1944 did cost us five pilots. Captain Dumoulin, squadron leader of my squadron, was killed by antiaircraft fire as he attacked the Gaiola bridge.

Between December 16, 1944, and the end of January, 1945, the "Roussillon" Group became fully outfitted with P-47 Thunderbolts. We were fighting-ready, able to rain fire and brimstone on Germany! Off we went to the airbase at the city of Luxeuil-les-Bains, named historically for its thermal baths, and not too far from the Swiss Alps. We were going to see combat on the Alsace front.

Imagine the weight of twelve to fifteen automobiles in one fighter plane. Our beloved Republic P-47 Thunderbolt came in

CHAPTER 11 *A Live Bomb for a Hockey Puck* 129

several models and the gross weight varied from thirteen thousand pounds to over twenty thousand pounds. The difference was the weight of armaments and supplemental fuel tanks, which were detachable, and there was that tank under the belly for long-distance flying.

With range varying between 550 miles and 2200 miles, she was a single-engine one-seater, and her Pratt & Whitney V-configured cylinders touted two thousand brake horsepower! The latest model cranked out twenty-two hundred horsepower, giving speeds from 430 miles per hour to 467 mph with a ceiling of thirty-five thousand feet. You could cross the whole country of France in just over one hour. The propeller was a four-bladed one whereas just three blades were very common.

Imagine, if you will, a P-47 machine-gunning the ground. This one Thunderbolt spat out over sixty bullets per second. Multiply this times twelve airplanes to represent seven thousand bullets in ten seconds! You'd do a great deal of damage. One or two passes over the target and the target was literally perforated through and through: German airplanes destroyed, not able to be used against us.

The Germans developed such a frightful shiver over our P-47s that when they saw us coming they'd scream, "*Achtung! Jabos!*" which is, "Look out! Fighter-bombers!" After dropping our bombs, we could engage their Messerschmitts and Focke-Wulf 190s.

*   *   *

Getting back to our missions over Italian soil, during the whole month of December, 1944, many missions got carried out with P-39s because at the beginning we only had four P-47s. More of them arrived in stages. By February, 1945, we had twenty-four P-47s for two squadrons of twelve each, and what a godsend. Both our squadrons could now set themselves to the task. I am taking out my Flight Log, where my Italian operations aboard the Cobra are recorded:

P-39   #186   *le 2 janvier : Bombard-t de Valdiéri (Italie)* {bombing mission over *Valdieri,* 02JAN, 1945}

P-39   #922   *le 3 janvier : Protection de Walrus* {bomber escort, 03JAN, 1945}

P-39   #917   *le 9 janvier : Bombardement du pont de Saorge* {bombed the Saorge bridge, 9JAN, 1945}

P-39   #917   *le 18 janvier : Bombardement à Isolabona, près de Pigna (Italie)*
{bombed Isolabona, near Pigna, 18JAN, 1945}

P-39   #918   *le 7 février : Bomb-t du pont de Dolcequa (Italie)* {bombed the Dolcequa bridge, 7FEB, 1945}

P-39   #358   *le 12 février : Bomb-t et mitraillage à Valdiéri* {bombing and strafing (machine-gunning) at the city of Valdieri, 12FEB, 1945}

These missions lasted from two to two and a half hours each.

Mission into Italy when I got Wounded

On February 25, 1945, my mission aboard the P-47 numbered 358 gave me some grief. It was strafing and bombing of the Caverns of Tinedio. These caverns were well-embedded in the mountains and I had to reduce my speed in order to keep my shooting accurate, squeezing between mountains which had staunch defenses. Their antiaircraft fire hit me along the fuselage and made a sieve out of my airplane. I took a bullet to the right calf. I tried to ignore this wound as my sole goal became piloting: I wanted to make it back home in one piece! It required focus to stay alert: verify tach, compass, altimeter. Keep the airspeed up, but economically, maintaining one eye on that fuel level.

Having landed, my weapons mechanic counted seventy-two points of impact on the wings and fuselage. He said to me, "You're a lucky man." He handed me a scrap of red metal. "You'll want to frame that." Indeed it still sits in a frame alongside my medals.

My weapons mechanic told me, "It's a chunk out of your left wing, which has a hole in it the size of my hand. That hole is right where the machinegun ammo box sits. Just an inch to the other side of that internal wing member, and the shot would have hit your munitions. Boom: explosion <u>and</u> losing a wing sure wouldn't give you any way to eject. You'd have been a fireball streaming to the ground."

He had helped me extricate myself from the cockpit to climb down. He was worried about my leg wound. "Oh, don't fret over that," I said. "It could have been worse."

He looked me in the eye as he said, "It looks like your machineguns got a workout. They're still hot and your ammo is almost gone."

In thanks, I gave him a pat on the shoulder. "I'm worn out. Come on, guy, let's get a drink. I'll give you a blow by blow account." All the mechanics hoped not to see damage to us and their airplanes. They worried about breakdowns. They worried about learning we'd bit the dust. They liked hearing about our missions, and this was recompense for the work they put into these planes. They seemed to listen intently to find out how each mission had gone. I found this to be perfectly natural, and God knows how we needed them, so it was really satisfying to describe our exploits to those guys. It was many a time that the *mécanos* [pronounce may-kah-NOH]* got anxious over a late arrival.

*   *   *

Meanwhile I got a pretty good grip on this P-47, as I learned that an eight ton airplane could indeed be engineered to handle well. What power! I wasn't yet authorized to fly the P-47 alongside the others because I lacked hours, both for aerobatics and formation-flying. I would need about ten more hours under my belt.

The Anatomy of Fear

Another episode: from one of my missions over Italy in a P-47 Thunderbolt. Never in my life have I felt <u>fear</u> to match that occasion's.

---

* In truth there were two groups. The other group: *armuriers* = weapons mechanics.

Fear, genuine *Fear*! It was part and parcel of being a fighter pilot. There are two different kinds of fear, and the one which is the most dreadful is the least anticipated: you're not ready, but you must maintain your composure and you must know how to choose a path of defense or a path of attack. The other type of fear would be one caused by something expected, so this case produces a foreseeable reaction. I speak of fears like the fear of dying, the fear of future consequences, versus the sudden nature of a stroke of bad luck. All this wore us down. All of this gnawed at us.

In the annals of fear there are extremes which are well-known, such as during a heart attack, hence the term "scared to death." Fear is a real thing. In yet other circumstances fear paralyses us. Can one overcome fear? According to the psychologists, yes. One needs strict discipline, a way to program his or her mind, so as not to bow down to emotion. We need to realize that when we're controlled by emotion our decisions can be erroneous. When faced with no time to think, we "fly" blind.

The Anatomy of Fear: Napalm Bomb

This being said, I can now describe for you the extreme fear I encountered on one of my last missions. We'd been briefed as to the fact that, for certain reasons, we'd be flying with Napalm bombs. One under each wing, these incendiary bombs burned at a high intensity. At the briefing we were told to release these bombs at low altitude so they would ricochet, making the fire spread by chain reaction when the bombs exploded. I wasn't too keen on the idea, but such was the order to be followed. Indeed this was the first time we were using this type of bomb. Why?

Our Intelligence Officer explained to us that this was a mission in collaboration with other squadrons we'd be joining forces with. It was all part of a major operation in an area near San Remo, Italy. At the briefing they told us there were a great many underground barracks. The area was huge, stretching many miles.

CHAPTER 11 *A Live Bomb for a Hockey Puck*

There were thousands of enemy troops hidden there, camouflaged, and we expected them to be launching a major offensive. Based on this knowledge we had to act quickly, to cause the most destruction in an attempt to cut off any possible escape. One pass, and all should be burned, all incinerated. Vicious as it was, it was war. We had to obey orders.

We got our best advice from the weapons mechanics: don't ever flip the release on a bomb unless you're sure it's going to fall. Theoretically the bomb couldn't explode under-wing, but once released we only had a fraction of a minute before it would. Compare this with normal bombs where they simply get released and a pilot has time to fly away before the blast. Dropped from high altitude, bombs like that take time to reach the ground: impact, explosion. These Napalm bombs were different.

There we were, off and running, with one diabolical bomb under each wing. Oh, how important, then, was an impeccable takeoff, and I didn't feel too confident during mine. I remember looking down on the enemy territory where we released these Napalm bombs: oh, what a true Hell. I wouldn't have wanted to be down there. It was dreadful, worse than flamethrowers.

Having returned almost to the base, we were relieved to think it was behind us. As we approached our landing strip, looking down we saw fire trucks readied for anything unexpected. Just as usual, we circled at an altitude of six hundred feet, passing over the control tower. In front of me, one plane veered off in preparation for landing, followed closely by another, and so forth until it got to be my turn. After I deployed my landing gear, my plane began shaking in a way I found troubling. All I could think was, "Hey, did the antiaircraft guns mess something up?"

I decided not to touch down. I pushed forward on the gas and gave another circle 'round, climbing slightly, giving me time to think. What should I do? My plane was still shaking. I was flying over the control tower again when, in my radio, I heard, "Code Red! Snowbee One*, you still have one bomb hanging under

---

* *My handle was truly in English: Snowbee One.*

your right wing! Perform Emergency Aerobatics Procedure over the lake."

"Snowbee One," I radioed back, "am heading for the lake." The lake was under a mile from the base.

At the lake I performed every conceivable aerobatic maneuver, special tricks they'd taught us, trying to shake that bomb loose. This went on for a solid quarter of an hour but that cursed bomb wanted nothing to do with it! Meanwhile the whole squadron had gathered on the field to watch. The commander got on the radio with me, consoling me. "Drabier, do some *forte glissade** maneuvers. Don't panic. It'll all come out ok." [Translator's note: at this point I suggested to Jacques that a "Yeah for you maybe!" would be cute. Jacques declined, saying humor was the furthest thing from his mind at that minute.] I gave a pedal-stroke to turn left as I pulled quickly on the stick. Ok. Still nothing. My fuel was depleting rapidly and with all this exercise I was sweating up a storm. Hyperbolic nervousness defines it. It seems incomprehensible, doesn't it? If this bomb goes off they'll never find any trace of me!

I thought through the instruction manual. I had two choices: A) eject, B) take on the mission of landing with the bomb, in prayer.

Sooooo, let us pray! I opted for plan B in considering two very important facts, even if my decision did represent, well, dementia. To die in combat or to die here, what would be the difference? But to save an airplane was important. We had so few. Pilots were always waiting for planes to arrive; acquiring planes was like squeezing blood from a stone.

I told the control tower I'd come in for a landing. By the grace of God, if I goof… well, we'll just see. I could already make out ambulances and firemen rushing about madly. I told myself that I had only one chance, not two; I wouldn't be able to take off again. I concentrated on my speed, trying to get it to the minimum, hoping for a pillow-soft landing. In a case like this, a pilot

---

* *maneuvers of inertia*

CHAPTER 11 *A Live Bomb for a Hockey Puck* 135

usually emptied his fuel tank over the lake, but my fuel was just sufficient to get me on the ground. Six hundred feet, 300 feet, 150 feet... I touched down ever so delicately, not having breathed throughout the whole enterprise.

Oof. A good <u>strong</u> breath was what I breathed now that my plane was on the ground. But I was rolling too fast! Thanks to the single rear wheel, which was fixed to prevent swerving, I rolled forward in a straight line. Suddenly, in disbelief, in front of me I saw the bomb hopping and skipping along, and it was going faster than I was! The bomb had finally detached and was sliding toward an empty area of the field. Quick, I squeezed on the brakes to cut my own speed in the wake of this infernal bomb. I just could not believe my eyes. Having released the pivot of my rear wheel, I engaged the left brake in a serious way. My P-47 pivoted fast, performing two pirouettes. It seemed as though I might rip the right wing to shreds, but better this maneuver than to hug up to that bomb which would surely explode any time now.

Finally my bomb came to a halt about three hundred feet in front of me, but without blowing up. Later, when the weapons mechanics retrieved it, they found the percussion tip detonator to be live. Luckily, as the bomb had detached, it had decided to slip and slide along the runway like a rock on a lake. If perchance it had managed to bump into something, or if it had bounced up onto its nose, the result would have been disastrous.

*   *   *

Needless to say, I was considered a hero. They congratulated me, but, before going to celebrate with my chums at the Mess, I excused myself to step aside and attend to one necessary and urgent obligation. You'll understand: it was a matter of wet underwear. You can well guess the reason.

P-47 Thunderbolt

War Pilot Memoirs: A Mirror on 1939

CHAPTER 12

Air Crafts: Not Identifiable

Before we close the book on my part in this Second World War, I must relate to you one encounter which came to pass. It's not written down in my flight log; it's not given anywhere in the annals of military aviation. The most logical reason for this would be the guarding of a military secret at the highest echelon of State, because the file belonged to Military Intelligence. Anyway, who would have believed my story?

I was the Patrol Leader with two other pilots. As was typically the case, the Leader got selected for being the one who knew the terrain the best. We were intercepted by three objects impossible to identify. They gave us a fright which defies description! These objects displayed a phenomenal speed and they had the appearance of silvery disks.

We were returning from a very arduous mission, more acute than the usual mission. We were low on fuel and completely out of munitions. About fifteen minutes out from the base at Salon-de-Provence near Marseille, we were flying low over the Alps. The sky was a pretty blue, it was around two o'clock in the afternoon, and the cloudless blue sky made it hard to judge how far away any flying object might be.

The pilot on my right signaled me by hand since we often

didn't use radios when near or behind enemy lines. He held up three fingers. He was indicating, way over there, to the right, the three objects. They were in a formation matching ours and they were heading the same direction we were. The pilot on my right made a sign at me in the form of a thumb-down, which was to say "enemy, not identifiable." The apparent dimension of these shiny, silvery disks was the size of a small coin when you hold it at arm's length between thumb and index finger.

Before each mission there was always a briefing where an Intelligence officer filled us in on anything new on the side of the Germans, such as a new weapon, a new airplane, or anything we might need to keep in mind during our mission. We'd heard nothing about anything which could resemble these objects.

In a case like this, the normal procedure would have been to evade and hide, hoping to avoid an attack. Especially since we didn't know what we were up against, we were vulnerable and without defenses. I wanted to get back to the base as quickly as possible: just ten minutes. If those shining things continued to follow us they'd get our antiaircraft fire from the guys on the ground. I'd only just completed this thought when abruptly two of the disks disappeared... literally evaporated, poof! Gone, vanished, and the only disk remaining made a sweeping circle, steering toward us, leaving a bright trail in its wake. The trail was blue, red, green, yellow and violet. Never have I seen fireworks to match it! With a speed really unknown to us... I wouldn't have had time to count to four... I saw it go between the mountains and underneath us. I was able, though, in a split second of time, to see a silvery disk which I judged to be about thirty-three feet in diameter going past at the speed of lightning before zigzagging upward. Poof! All gone! Not surprisingly, the other pilots swerved suddenly upward on my left and on my right, screaming, "What the Devil is this? What do we do?"

It was hard for me to get them back into formation; we were really shaken up, as if a diabolical monster were going to swallow us. There remained no more than five minutes before getting

CHAPTER 12 *Air Crafts: Not Identifiable*

to the base, and luckily so, since the instruments on our dashboards were dancing around like spinning toys. My Sperry gyrocompass was turning backwards at high speed. As for the other instruments, needles were going from left to right giving no indication of what they should. When that disk had gone past at the speed of light underneath my plane, there had been some type of green glow, illuminating my cockpit for just the duration of a second. I got an electric shock all over my body!

We came out of our aerobatics and regrouped into formation, and it was at this precise moment that I experienced a sensation of being turned upside down; I felt a chaos created in my mind. After landing I learned that the same phenomena had occurred in the cockpits of the other two pilots. The one exception was that they had not experienced the green glow.

*   *   *

Many years would go by before I came to realize what this light signified, this light which launched the out-of-control spinning of instruments at the moment the disk flew by. Definitively, it was a very, very strong magnetic force, unknown in the annals of Physics. Of course it was necessary to change out the instruments in the dashboards of all three planes, to the great surprise of the Air Corps.

Just as was customary we went to give a report on the mission, noting the event which had befallen us, with no doubt in our minds that such a report would really shake them up. In the 1940s the word "Ovni" (*Objet Volant Non Identifié*, the equivalent of the English-speaking "Ufo" for Unidentified Flying Object) was not known. People around the world, including French speakers, said "foo fighter" instead. This came perhaps from *faux* (false) or *feu* (fire) or *fou* (crazy). There was a surrealistic comic strip beginning in 1935 which lasted over thirty years, and in the 1938 Big Little Book <u>Smokey Stover the Foo Fighter</u>, Smokey says, "Where there's foo, there's fire."

As we presented our report to the group commander, he looked at us for a bit without even lifting an eyebrow. Having read our report he shook his head, grabbed the phone and dialed the official sawbones of the base, saying, "Doctor, I'm sending you three of my guys just back from a mission. I'm worried about them. I think they're really exhausted, to the extent of having collective hallucinations! They gave me one bizarre report. Can you take a look at them?" No quicker said than done.

We were more than a little upset over his sending us to the infirmary. We were suspended from flying for three days to undergo special treatment. Mandatory rest and relaxation, but with good eats: beef-steaks to get us back on our feet and to restore our morale. They persuaded us not to include any of these reports in any part of the squadron's work log. This went to such an extent that I firmly believe not one word ever got transmitted to Central Command.

Just to assure our silence, they had us sign papers confirming we'd never seen anything special, confirming the necessity of forgetting this episode by reason of military secrecy. Believe it, or not!

Nothing to match this ever came my way again.

*　　　　*　　　　*

Today, 65 years later, my knowledge goes a bit deeper. Many years after the war, when I started having visions, having flashbacks, I developed telepathy. Mentally I was able to receive information from the beyond, to the extent that I sincerely began to question my perception and recall, to question my sanity. I consulted a psychiatrist to find out what was happening to me. After some exams which were plenty complex and thorough, I was deemed sane and in good health. For years I researched the matter to learn more. It's a long story which I'll tackle in an upcoming work, for we're broaching a subject which is very extensive, with a considerable amount of documentation, of real contacts, with numerous authentic photographs taken by people of solid reputations.

CHAPTER 12 *Air Crafts: Not Identifiable*

For more than twenty years after the war I never once had another encounter with UFOs. All of a sudden, while I was residing in Los Angeles, California, it all started up again: the saucers, plus visitations, contacts and visions. It was then that I decided to dig deeply into the subject with every means at my disposal. This now makes forty-five years I've researched the paranormal and extraterrestrials.

The Encounter

War Pilot Memoirs: A Mirror on 1939

CHAPTER 13

Chivalry in the Skies

Throughout the month of February, 1945, I flew missions over Italy: protecting allied convoys, blowing up bridges, bombing ports and most particularly taking out antiaircraft emplacements, which was a delicate operation since you had to be swift enough to destroy the cannons before the cannons could destroy you! This was like the game of staring someone in the eyes to see who blinks first. In order to aim properly we had to fly straight, that is, straight ahead without veering for a certain time, which gave time to the enemy on the ground to fire on us. When they were quicker, the inevitable exploding of an airplane gave a pilot not even enough time to make the sign of the cross from his forehead to his chest.

In addition, we escorted bombers, including those huge Flying Fortresses and Liberators, as they proceeded to targets. Our job was to keep German fighters off of them. Some bombers* were armed to the teeth with large caliber machineguns: pivoting turrets atop the fuselage, underneath, not to forget one at the end of the tail and bubble windows in each side of the fuselage. We, of course, had the advantage of being able to maneuver in counter-attack and pursue the German fighters. This let the

---

* More B-24 "Liberators" than B-17 "Flying Fortresses" were produced, yet the catchphrase of the latter seems to have caught on. There were many others in the B- series.

"fortresses" continue on, in formation, destined for some city... and its destruction.

Stationed at Luxeuil, a French city that's due west of Basel which is in northernmost Switzerland, our missions now went over German soil, or over the country of Luxemburg, or over the Ardennes Mountains (famous for its Battle of the Bulge), or farther north around Bastogne, a city in Belgium. On Wednesday, April 11, 1945, I took off in my P-47 Thunderbolt, number 919, for a bomber protection mission over Germany. The mission would last two hours and ten minutes. We were escorting B-17s or B-24s from an American squadron as they headed for a large weapons factory at Mungentum. The factory was well protected by antiaircraft cannons, so we were being plenty careful. Before the antiaircraft fire had even begun, all of a sudden German fighters came raining down on our backs! A guy had to pick one, before he picked you, and with luck bring him down. I was firing profusely, really trying to defend the bombers, when I perceived that there were fewer German planes in the sky.

I had no idea who'd been hit, but I could see planes on fire everywhere. Unfortunately many of these burning planes were ours. There were two of the big bombers burning. Several of the German planes were too; they'd been hit by gunfire from the "flying fortresses." In front of me the sky was black, obscured by clouds of smoke, and antiaircraft fire was darkening it too. I became a target, being out of ammo, so I had to think fast. What to do? In my mind, I was cornered: if I tried to flee, I'd be shot down. I had no munitions, no way to defend myself against the remaining German planes which were still attacking our bombers. The bomber which I was escorting flew onward, but I saw two Focke-Wulfs bearing down on me! I radioed the "fortress" to let me duck under his left wing. I was depleted, I could not defend myself, so I tilted my wings to get his attention as I tucked myself under his wing. If the Germans came after me, at least I'd have cover, and the Krauts would have to get in close to hit me, seeing as how they'd have bullets raining on them from the turrets.

CHAPTER 13 *Chivalry in the Skies*

My plan worked. The first Focke-Wulf missed me then flew under the bomber only to take a hit and go down in flames. The second one as well got cut in half then burst into flames as he fell. This was the last of the German planes. Yippee! I radioed a "Thanks, guys!" to the Americans. From their side, on the same frequency, I heard laughter and shouts of joy too. I broke off from under-wing to head back to base, safe and sound. I never had the chance to thank those guys in person for saving my skin.

The Dogfight where MY BUTT gets Spared

The strength of German aviation was now losing its plumage. To put the timeline in perspective, it would be only weeks later when, on Monday, April 30th, 1945, Hitler would commit suicide in Berlin. Less and less often did we see German planes patrolling in large groups. We'd see just three to four airplanes at a time, sometimes just one or two on reconnaissance. We knew the Krauts to be merciless; they behaved as desperados, as savage men beyond hope. They machine-gunned parachutists during descent. Our pilots, once ejected, became vulnerable and powerless to defend themselves.

Yet we knew the German fighter pilots to be skilled, superior to us thanks to longer experience. We had our champions, yes indeed, like Francis Gabreski, an American pilot of Polish descent, who scored fourteen kills in his P-47. There was Pierre Clostermann, a Frenchman, in his Spitfire Tempest with thirty-three kills, France's most decorated pilot.

Collectively, others shot down hundreds of Kraut airplanes. Many were flying P-47s but others flew P-51 Mustangs. These were ferocious combats, so much so that we compared them to when the "Spads" (the aircraft manufacturer, 1913-1919, called *Société Pour l'Aviation et ses Dérivés*) of the Great War had flown against the Red Baron. Back then, they had gone so far as to call that combat "noble", that is: possessing a certain *chevalerie*, said chivalry being acknowledged on both sides of enemy lines.

Sadly this chivalry wasn't found in our second World War, but then came the day when, within <u>my</u> experience, an exception produced itself, contrary as this may be to popular consensus. There was a squadron, a subset of World War Two German aces, calling themselves "vonRichthofens", who perpetuated this *noblesse*, this etiquette, in the name of the Red Baron.

Sunday, April 8, 1945; flying P-47 serial number 386. It was a bombing mission, a successful one, on a train near Hausach; we were three fighters. Having dropped our bombs we were on our way up to fifteen thousand feet. Out of nowhere two Messerschmitt 109s appeared, and, wide-eyed, I saw them face to face with us! They'd caught us off guard and sent one of my two compatriots flaming to the Earth. A fierce combat ensued. I perceived, and correctly so, much skill on the German side; these pilots were true acrobats and their style of approach was little understood by us. I began imitating them, trying to replicate their methodology, but alas my aerobatics were not on their level. I was far less effective, less efficient. Each time I managed to get the Kraut plane into my gun sight, I fired… but my adversary would spin away, unscathed, in complex gyrations.

I was sweating up a storm. Beads of sweat ran into my eyes affecting my vision, so much so that I lost all sight of my one remaining colleague. I radioed to him an appeal to get this Kraut off my butt. Unfortunately, my colleague was not close at hand: no response by radio, nowhere in sight. Suddenly I saw tracer bullets whizzing past, meaning this Kraut was behind me trying to poke holes into me like a sieve! I disengaged. I performed a barrel-roll while diving, knowing he would not follow. Indeed, he veered off to the side. Classic maneuvers were three barrel-rolls then disengage toward the sky, or two and a half barrel-rolls then disengage toward the soil, but I did a single barrel-roll and disengaged upward to chase him. A highly skilled adversary can actually barrel-roll with you, behind you at six o'clock, firing as he goes; luckily this would not be the case. The magnificent motor of my P-47 gained speed for me hard and fast, as I revved her up

CHAPTER 13 *Chivalry in the Skies*

to the limit. I found myself straight under him with an up-angle of 45 degrees. I got him in my sights and fired on my adversary. Suddenly I ran out of ammo! Crap, I almost had him! My adversary disengaged in a grand circle; I could not see him any more.

There I was, alone, thinking surely now I was busted, that my number was up. He had the upper hand. My only chance might be to dive hard and fast in an attempt to lose him. Impossible; my altitude's too low. Such a maneuver would take me into the Alps. With the German hot on my tail, I experienced a whirlwind of memories: childhood, my fiancée... all this flashed before my eyes. I uttered my final prayer. I crossed myself in good Catholic fashion, knowing the end was here, not "near"; it was here.

I was flying straight ahead, simply maintaining one thousand feet of altitude, not even bothering to look to see where the Messerschmitt was. Straight ahead. Simply, straight ahead. Very tense, I awaited the *coup de grâce*, a death quite certain. My eyes were fixed as I prayed.

In a stark instant, there on my right, wing tip to wing tip, I saw the German Cross on the fuselage of my adversary! I could not believe my eyes, as I also noted the insignia of the Red Baron. The German pilot was so close that I could see the whites of his eyes; he had lifted his goggles up to the front of his helmet. With a "thumb up" sign, with what must have been a grand smile on his face... is he signaling goodbye? Yes, incredible as it seemed, my adversary was over there waving at me! Then, fast as lightning, he disengaged and made for the horizon without any other fanfare. I lost my breath. Wide-eyed in haggard fashion, not yet able to regroup, there trickled upon my cheeks: tears.

Forever emblazoned in my memory is that vonRichthofen insignia, sign of that infamous German squadron of aces. In a definitive moment of my life, I met a champion, and I would love to know who he was. By a gesture of chivalry he had spared me from certain death. He had realized that I had no more cartridges and that a combat mustn't become a murder. Do you, dear Reader, now agree that gallant chivalry did survive in German aviation?

* * *

I got assigned a mission against the artillery at the town of Verdon, on the peninsula called Pointe de Grave on the Atlantic coast of France, across the inlet from the city of Royan, just north of and downriver from the city of Bordeaux. This newfound luxury of flying westward across our own soil, from bases like Luxeuil near Switzerland, was appreciated by all the French pilots. This mission was on Thursday the 19th of April, 1945, aboard P-47 Thunderbolt, serial number 815: bombing and strafing of Pointe de Grave. We used to call this kind of site *des poches* [pronounce day PUHshh], which meant "pockets" of last resistance, noting this was just a few weeks before Berlin would fall and "V.E. Day", for Victory in Europe, would be declared. On other missions we had bombed the cities of Royan and St. Georges de Didonne, both located near the port city of La Pallice, a primary port for German submarines. These subs were thought to be a potential escape route for Hitler, so that's why the port of La Pallice had been designated for us to attack.

Although most of the Germans knew the war was lost, they had nonetheless strengthened their defenses around La Pallice to the maximum. There was artillery of every caliber, spanning an area of over sixty miles in diameter. The closer you got to La Pallice the denser their defenses were. In places there was an installation every hundred yards, and the magnitude of this firepower aimed at us formed an almost impenetrable barrier. Plenty of our planes got shot down here, whereas I, the ever-loving lucky duck, limped back to base again and again with a sieve for an airplane! One time I brought back a P-47 Thunderbolt which was lacking two cylinders but stubbornly functioned still. These ever-ready P-47s brought me back plenty of times to the base, safe and soundly whole. That particular day, when I got back from my mission, I kissed my *oiseau* [pronounce wah-ZOHH], my "bird."

*　　　*　　　*

CHAPTER 13 *Chivalry in the Skies*

At long last the few remaining Germans surrendered and accounts got settled. The city of Royan, well known to me since I'd spent carefree vacations there as a child, was eighty-five percent destroyed. Aunt Lucie's house, near the supply tank filled with natural gas, was pulverized when a bomb exploded that tank. What a traumatic event for my family, and what a drama for me! "Adieu" to my childhood memories within those walls.

"Noblesse oblige"

War Pilot Memoirs: A Mirror on 1939

CHAPTER 14

Post-War Wedding Bells: Wine, not Beer

I got a letter from England, from the hand of my fiancée Vera, asking, "When in the world are we going to get married?" We'd been engaged since 1942. This called for thoughtful reflection, since my unit was on the verge of being sent off to occupied Germany, to the city of Trier, twenty miles east of the country of Luxemburg, in the Moselle Valley. This was an occupied zone designated French.

Truth be told I knew I needed to make a decision but I'd formulated some plans to visit Paris and see my family, particularly my Aunt Tino. I kept asking myself if I'd find everyone alive! Would I still find the people I'd known, situated where I'd known them? What had gone on during the occupation of Paris? All these questions needed answers before I could set a date with my fiancée.

Leave Request Granted for Paris

Late May, 1945. I had racked up over a week of time for liberty. Leaving behind my P-47 Thunderbolt (my "jug")* at the city of Strasbourg in France where it would remain in service, I

---

* In the era of carburetors and such, individual airplanes behaved differently. It was typical that one pilot would fly one plane. My letter "V" as nose art stood for "Vera", my fiancée.

boarded an airplane called "*Le Goéland*", "The Seagull", as a passenger for Paris.

Arriving Paris with abundant tears in my eyes, I took a cab to get to the apartment where I used to be so very happy. I made it back to the street "rue du Général de Maud'huy" in the eighteenth arrondissement, to Aunt Betty's apartment which was still there; the building had not been struck by the bombs of war. Behind this building I still saw the "Zone", the poor people's ghetto where destitute people lived in shacks made of cardboard, and for windows and doors they used burlap or jute-sacks. This "Zone" was only a few hundred yards behind the fine buildings of the 18th arrondissement.

Still in my Army Air Corps uniform, I located Tino and Aunt Betty! They were very proud of me. They embraced me, ha! ...before setting themselves to cajoling me. We had so, so much to catch up on, but above all they wanted to spoil me first, so they offered me sumptuous foods they'd been able to hoard. All rations were still obtained by tickets, and worse yet the gals had to stand in line for hours at the little grocer's shop for the bit of bread allotted to them, plus a small container of skim milk. It had that disagreeable blue tint associated with skim milk. Butter was very scarce, unless you were one of those enterprising people who got butter from some farm in the Somme region and sold it on the black market with exorbitant markup. There always are people who range from crafty to dishonest that sell black market goods with exorbitant markup. It was explained to me that life had been hard. During the occupation plenty of folks rummaged German trashcans, since the Krauts wasted plenty and just tossed it away. Some Parisians were so hard up they did this just to survive. Others gleaned from farm fields.

Before going on leave I had been remunerated a small sum as an advance. Part was paid as I went on leave and the rest would be paid when finally discharged. This time spent in Paris was the essence of blessed liberty: I went to the movies, I pampered myself with food and drink in restaurants, I savored each and every

CHAPTER 14 *Post-War Wedding Bells: Wine, not Beer*   153

moment. I went to the park, I visited friends who had survived, and I made what would be my last climb up the Eiffel Tower.

By early June my leave was up, so I went to Trier in Germany to begin my duty with the occupation forces. I had been promoted to Second Lieutenant and I'd become chummy with Major Nodet, squadron leader of Fighter Group "Roussillon", now that we were an occupation force. With Major Nodet, then, I shared the fact that I wanted to marry in England. "Bravo," he said to me. "You deserve this. No problem. How much time do you need? How can I help?" Great. I could see my rank and seniority and decorations came with privileges. He gave me almost a month.

To get to England I had to go in a Dakota C-47 (number 842), a military passenger plane. So, the 8th of June, 1945, a Friday, saw me bound for Horsham, England. Once on the ground in London I took a local train into the county called Sussex. Vera was wrapping up her studies in Nursing, so on this day she was at the hospital. Since she did not have the liberty of coming to meet me at the train station, to the hospital I went, excited as could be. She knew I was to arrive on this date, since I had written, but she did not know what time to expect me.

I showed up at the hospital reception desk, pretty as a rooster in my dress uniform. Alongside the entranceway there stood a flower boutique and I snagged the biggest bouquet of red roses they had. Anxious and impatient, I had to wait in the lobby since the hospital's rules disallowed going in. My heart was thumping *grand coup*; it had been three years since I'd seen my fiancée!

On my left an automatic door opened. I saw my fiancée in her so wonderfully white uniform, in her cute little bonnet which all the nurses wore in those days. Time stood still: emotional recovery time, then we threw ourselves into each others arms. The precious moment got interrupted by a "hum, hum." It was Madame the hospital supervisor who was coming toward us and shaking her head. She said, "That's not permitted here." In England it was not considered proper to embrace in public, and I was not yet up to speed on protocol. A certain British puritan ethic, which has been there forever, edified by the rules of royalty. Oops!

After all, having been apart for three long years, I felt I had the right. So, there in front of God and everybody, nurses and doctors alike, I simply avoided being bothered. And as for the matron, Madame the hospital supervisor? Well, sorry. Just then a doctor with a complacent smile walked by, and he said, "Good chap, lucky you," as he went on his way.

Vera was blushing, flushed red with joy, and she said to the other nurses, "This is my French hero. He's a fighter pilot, you know." They all applauded and shared in her happiness.

We sneaked off to an adjacent room to continue hugging and kissing and talking over all kinds of things. Most particularly, we spoke about getting married.

Finally Vera finished her shift and we took a bus to go to her house. She said, "I called my mom from the hospital. She's fixing something special."

"Great," was my response. Near the bus stop, on the corner, there was a florist, so I quickly bought a bundle of marguerites. These were really in season that June, so the florist had plenty. Making our way to Vera's house I could not help noticing how much alike these houses looked, all lined up side-by-side in a typically English style. These were simple houses for factory workers, for retirees, or just for folks of modest means.

Vera's mother was overjoyed to know I'd arrived. Having been warmly welcomed I could not help but enjoy the fresh smell of the nice clean house. The inside was a humble setting with simple furniture. The ambiance was pleasant, and several paintings plus some family photos adorned the walls.

One of these photographs, bigger than the others, drew my special attention. It was a photo of a ship. Right away I got an explanation from Mr. Wells, my having posed to him the question. The infamous *HMS Terrible* had been involved in the "Boxer Days" campaign on China, August, 1900, when the Eight-Nation Alliance had gone to the defense of their own in Peking, now

CHAPTER 14   *Post-War Wedding Bells: Wine, not Beer*

called Beijing. He had worked in the ship's engine room stoking the furnaces with coal, but he often had been the gunner for cannon "number two" aboard the *HMS Terrible*. There always were, he told me, maritime foot-soldiers onboard who appreciated any and all support, this part of his story being 1899 to 1900 during the war of British versus Boers in South Africa. With the help of fifteen other sailors, Albert Wells had detached the cannons from ship's pivots and transported the cannons to the city of Durban, using them against Boer insurgents attacking Ladysmith, South Africa.

Mr. Wells, having lit his pipe, said to me, "Jake, let's get to the pub for a beer, since dinner isn't quite ready yet."

Then Vera chimed in, "Go on. All his mates are there. Dad will be so proud to show you off."

In the meantime the front door opened and there appeared Darcy and Connie to welcome me. They seemed relieved to see me in one piece. Vera cornered her sister toward the kitchen, as Albert grabbed Darcy's hand in turn and said, "Let's get to the pub for a beer... with Frenchy! He'll regale us with his exploits." There went the three of us, and we all took to each other very nicely. For me it was a down-home, family feel which had been truly lacking in my life. I felt comfortable. This family helped me understand England a bit better, with its customs and traditions which I barely knew.

We set our wedding date: June 11, 1945, a Monday, at a church in the city of Horsham, Sussex. It was a Church of England. This Church is quite similar to the Catholic Church, but I was distressed to learn that the marriage of an Anglican and a Catholic did cause certain problems, especially on the Catholic side. Since I only had three weeks of liberty left, a quick decision was called for: it would be an Anglican ceremony, which much pleased my future wife's family. I, being of the Catholic faith, had to get permission from the Archbishop of Canterbury. Only he could give the go-ahead which would see me accepted into their Church.

Vera and I could at long last be united. But with the war just ending, a pretty bridal dress could just not be bought. It became, then, the family's duty to put one together. As for me, things were simpler since I could wear my uniform. Gallant in the appropriate way, I set myself to planning the festivities and the booze. Ahh, thus the opportunity presented itself that I should "pin" a petite revenge on my father-in-law, Albert, who loved his beer so much. I must confess, in that domain of beer, he was quite invincible.

Hey, it was my wedding and I decided not to serve beer but some fine wine instead. Since Albert had always succeeded in sending me to roll under the table with his beer, now I could get revenge with wine and champagne. Rest assured, my plan worked. In due turn, I sent him to roll under the table. I was plenty happy, too, with the way things were progressing in general with my little bride.

One heartache did prevail, though: no member of my family could attend. Of course this had been a rapid decision and, given the great distance, my family could not make it. My parents were still in Indochina, modern South Vietnam. My uncles and aunts were on business trips, etcetera, not to forget the general difficulty of postwar traveling.

My leave drew near its end. I had to get back to Germany and, during the occupation, complete my tour of duty. My wife, Vera, still had six months to go to complete her studies in Nursing. By that time, six months hence, I too was to have ended my military service.

CHAPTER 14 *Post-War Wedding Bells: Wine, not Beer* 157

My wedding of June 11, 1945,
to Vera Wells, in Horsham, Sussex, UK.

War Pilot Memoirs: A Mirror on 1939

CHAPTER 15

Small Game Hunts in German Forests & Reports of Japanese Acts

In France, these were days of catching our breath, for there was a great deal of cleaning up to do. We had a new, yet provisional, government which was doing its best to guide and control its people, in particular to control the Communist Party now experiencing a rapid expansion.

I took a P-47 Thunderbolt to get to Trier, West Germany, where getting back to work was an uphill battle for me. I knew that my military career was coming to an end, that I had a civilian life in my future, and that I had left my poor little wife all alone. Getting this military job done was important, though. I lived in the home of an elderly German couple; he was a railroad retiree and she was an admirable *bourgeoise*, a strong figure of a city gal. Their daughters were ages 19 and 17. The eldest was impatiently awaiting the return of her fiancé, an SS soldier who was still being held in a prison camp. The house was large, so my subordinate officer and I each had a private room. Four soldiers guarded us, as well as this family, against any little uprisings or riots or fanatical acts as we, the occupying forces, coerced the Germans into a new, non-Nazi, way of life.

There was a provisional airbase set up for our squadron. We found two Messerschmitt 109s, intact! We took turns flying those beasts, so renowned for their in-flight comportment. We wanted to experience firsthand how this formidable airplane functioned, to discover its secrets. I simply recall how, even as a young and slender man, the damned cockpit was so tight I twisted one shoulder forward to fly comfortably. The months of June, July and August, 1945, went by practically without flying our own planes: no missions.

This was just like vacation. We went hunting in the woods and boating on the Moselle River to catch some fish. For me, this time in Germany was a closing of the military chapter of my life.

One day I got a telegram from Horsham, England, telling me Albert Wells had died at age 77. This was, of course, a tough blow to me and the whole family. I had profound friendship with, and a great admiration for, this man. I could appreciate his past and I loved him dearly.

According to my flight log, my last flight of a P-47 Thunderbolt was 18 OCT 1945. In flight logs, by the way, red underlines mean military missions; civilian planes, or military planes flown on non-military missions, are not underlined. I had just received my discharge papers, wrapping up a phase as war pilot and returning me happily to civilian life. The war behind me, I could count almost six years of military service. Statisticians tell us that over two thirds of the pilots like me, those who started early in the war, did not live past 1945. I consider myself blessed with a favorable destiny to have survived. I also think it is evidence of a Universal Force that we were able to quash a madman like Hitler.

During our occupation of Germany we didn't fly much because our mission was to aid German authorities in converting over to a new system, to foster cooperation with the Allies in reconstructing their cities and their economy.

An impatience took me, an impatience for getting back into civilian life, and an impatience to see my parents who were in

CHAPTER 15   *Small Game Hunts in German Forests...*

Indochina, modern day South Vietnam. What had happened to them during these long years of separation?

*   *   *

Having reestablished contact with my parents I came to learn the horrors they'd had to undergo during Japanese occupation. All Europeans living in Indochina had been under the Japanese yoke: with minor exceptions, no one could leave his or her home. Food-shopping duties and such were carried out by domestic servants who, themselves, were monitored by soldiers of the Empire.

My parents managed to survive by pretending to support the Vichy Government back in France. This Vichy Government, based in southern France, was hard to comprehend for the Japanese, or for anyone for that matter. In northern France, truly "occupied" territory of the Germans, people faced firing squads on the weakest of evidence, whereas in the South, with "Vichy", there was at least some degree of a French buffer. There existed a degree of "back patting" psychology on the part of the Vichy French. They managed to soften the Germans' decisions in every shape and form, even as to executions and such. The French ladies' charm came into play to save French lives, since German officers were easily swayed by romance. We did have a bad word, though, *milicieux* (malicious in a military sense) for Vichyists who were German supporters, worse to us than the Nazis themselves.

On occasion, my parents were authorized to go, under escort, to the village church for services or to the movie theater. They had to put on airs of accepting these Japanese, of acting as propagandists. Notwithstanding all of this, there came a day when my father quite literally came close to losing his head.

*   *   *

An officer of the Empire of Japan, a young and overzealous one, had just replaced his predecessor, such a change in assignments happening every two months or so. This new officer had in his possession a letter I had written my parents from England. This letter, which I had entrusted to the Red Cross for delivery, had been found in the hands of a British Intelligence officer who regretfully had been discovered then killed. In the letter I had been prudent enough not to reveal anything, luckily, but the letter did show me to be in the Free French Air Force. The Japs considered me a traitor, being a pilot for other than the Vichy Government, so of course my dad was the father of a traitor. This young officer showed the letter to my father and said, "You know, I can execute you on the spot, with no other protocol or trial, no problem."

My father didn't let this rattle him. Calmly he said, "Do what you think is right. What is important to me is to know my son's ok." The young officer didn't answer, and the thing which saved my father was a true miracle. You see, this young officer, who spoke very good French, was studying in Japan to be a lawyer, so he had a certain interest in talking with my father who was a defense lawyer. They had discussions comparing jurisprudence in Japan to that of France.

This young officer had a few more things to say. "You're lucky," he said to my dad, "to be under my control since it was my men who intercepted the letter. No one else knows about it. If perchance the letter had been intercepted by the General Brigade, I would have been ordered to kill you on the spot." Cordially the officer offered my dad a glass of *sake*, their favorite cocktail. I believe this young officer respected my father very much. The officer even made the remark, "I don't like the Germans, and I hope your son will kill as many as he can over there."

Well, this was in the past. What was important to me, from the bottom of my heart, was the joyful thought of seeing my parents alive. They had finally departed Indochina, leaving all their worldly possessions behind, because, after capitulating, the Japanese had left the French with no arms or firearms in the midst of a hateful population, a population converted to communism after a long occupation. The arrival of the Russians in the function of propagandists for a communist regime created confusion among the people, who were nowhere near understanding what this regime was offering them. The people wanted, above all, independence and separation from France with its principal of colonialism. Thus began the Vietminh, which was a movement for the reclaiming of Indochinese independence.

So my parents, seeing what was going on, fled Saigon in a hurry before things could take a turn for the worse and leave them trapped. They set up housekeeping again near the town of Angoulins-sur-mer (Angoulins by the Sea) in the Department of Charente Maritime on the Atlantic coast of France. The quaint village of Angoulins-sur-mer is about twelve miles from La Rochelle and it's right on the water.

Where was I at this time? I'd just walked out of the Air Ministry office in Paris where they'd paid me my final paycheck, plus a bonus for my five and a half years, and they'd given me my discharge papers. I went straight to the shopping district called *Galleries Lafayette* to buy me a suit and a dress hat, some clothes, a suitcase... hey, I was a new man!

Back to civilian life.
A well-deserved drink with my parents.

War Pilot Memoirs: A Mirror on 1939

CHAPTER 16

Back in France, & Surprise: Maritime Saigon

Back Home to Look for Work

Having spent a week in Paris with my aunts Betty and Tino, I now boarded a train for La Rochelle, a six hour trip. The sea air of the Atlantic and the saline smell refreshed my lungs. A bus got me to Angoulins-sur-mer where I recognized the Post Office, the baker's shop and of course the precious old front gate to the courtyard of our house. With a trembling hand, I rang. I could see through the window how Mom, my *Maman**, was scurrying to open the door. I had tears in my eyes and my dear little *Maman* did too; this was a hug which lasted awhile! To me she seemed to have aged very much in five years, but she still had her sparkling little eyes which were shining. "Jacki, my little one, come in. Your father will be back from the office just any moment. We stashed away a good bottle of red wine, produced the year you enlisted, and we promised ourselves to open it only when you got back."

My father arrived. My God, how he looked bony and old. His hair was all white and he had just enough sparsely to cover his head. A long patriarchal accolade followed. As he ended it, he said, "Well, my boy, how are YOU? You look to be strong and healthy."

* Pronounce mah-MÃ where Ã = the "en-" nasal of "envelope."

I replied, "But as for you, we'll have to kill the fatted calf to get you back on your feet. You're nothing but skin and bones."

His excuse was, "Yep, I know, but give me time. I'm recovering from an imposed fasting of four years under the Japs."

Papa opened that infamous bottle of wine, a Bordeaux from Talence (Southwest France, Gironde Department, Aquitaine region). We clinked a toast and sang "*Vive la France et à son futur*" (Long Live France, and Here's to her Future). Out of the corner of my eye I saw Papa looking at me, a luminescent expression on his face, so I think he was proud of "my boy."

He'd had to sell his law office in Saigon. In the city of La Rochelle, to which he commuted by bus, he was renting space for his practice. For the time being things were going kind of slowly. He said to me, "You know, I'm going to have to quit someday, for health reasons. Getting old is no picnic, Big Guy!" Liquidating some other holdings in La Rochelle would be part of it. Papa had an enterprise that provided crushed oyster shells for poultry feed and for paving roads, driveways and even landing strips for airplanes.

This town of Angoulins-sur-mer had been a key part of my second childhood, age 13 to 16. Everybody in the village knew me: the Château brothers, whose family ran the little bakery shop that smelled so good, the Moinard family (he was the mayor of La Rochelle), all of whose kids were married by now. They had a grand house and magnificent grounds where, from father (mayor) to son, they were beekeepers. These bees produced a honey that made you think of perfume, and it had an excellent taste. The Belot family, fishermen, furnished the best oysters in the world, the flat cultivated oysters of Charente Maritime called *huîtres de Marennes*. And the Belots brought in shrimp: "Pink, or grey!" The pink ones were littler. Oh, yes, I remember the fish market with sardines poked into a funnel-shaped newspaper. Plastic bags had not been invented yet.

So here I was, having set up housekeeping at my parents' home, and I must admit the return to a family life was something to be savored. It's just that my little wife was not there with us, since she still had to wrap up her Nursing exams in England.

CHAPTER 16 *Back in France, & Surprise...* 167

This was a period when time moved slowly for me. While waiting, I looked for work, just as did all the guys discharged from the service. It was no piece of cake to find a job in a France undergoing reconstruction.

Times were tough. In 1946 our food still came to us via ticket control, so the black market was in its glory days. You couldn't get butter, and an eighth of a pound of meat per week was a person's allotment via tickets. Milk was blue, and not only had the dairymen taken out all the cream but, dishonest as it was, they'd added water. You had to wait long hours in line to buy anything. We were lucky to know fishermen, friends of Papa's, who took care of us. To take advantage of this we had to get up at dawn, go down to the port and meet the boats coming in with their holds full of fish. These hearty guys went out in the middle of the night to fish the deep waters, which yielded a bountiful harvest. Of course there were wholesale buyers who tried to work their way to the front of the line and get the biggest catch. Fishermen supplied restaurants too, where they were better paid for making the delivery. It was the leftovers of this feeding frenzy that the little man, like me, had to settle for. Still, these fishermen gave us good quality fish. It was worth the trouble.

My father would suffer a cerebral hemorrhage in 1959, rendering him hemiplegic; he'd lose the use of his right side, and his power of speech. This would devastate my mother. His cigarette smoking was what stands out in my mind; he smoked like a smokestack his whole life. Sadly, ever since the war of 1914, that is World War I, my father had only had the use of one lung. He was in the Battle of Verdun where the Germans used mustard gas. While he and other soldiers were charging with bayonets, he lost his mask. Before finding, on a corpse, another mask to put on, he breathed in enough gas to burn his lungs. Anyway, smoking the way he did surely didn't help his overall health. My poor, courageous Papa died of a heart attack in 1961 at the age of seventy-four.

* * *

I had a lot of trouble finding work. The funds from my military discharge were diminishing rapidly and I did not want to depend on my parents. A lucky star did appear: there came a day when Uncle Leon Nant, Aunt Betty's husband, paid us a visit. His pretext was getting his wife out of the Parisian congestion to offer her fresh sea air and a visit with her sister, my mother.

Providence is Looking out for Me

At the table with some hearty *pastis** in front of us, my uncle told me, "Jacques, it hurts me to see you looking so hard for work with no luck." I'd explained all my attempts which kept bringing me home empty-handed. "Ahh," he said, lifting his eyebrows, "would you like to go back to Indochina?" He had a sincere smile on his face. I had not pondered whether the whole world was as sluggish as France in getting back up and running, but surely things were bad all over. "No," he said, "things are picking up just fine in Indochina. Next week I'm headed back there. I'll check up on work for you." It should be said that Uncle Leon was one of the biggest import-export merchants in Indochina. He'd come to Europe to nurture his business, contributing to the economic recovery. He was respected, well connected and had influence in many branches of commerce. What he really had was the gift of gab as a promoter; many ranked him in a class of his own. His particular innate philosophy appealed to Orientals.

Abruptly, without preparation, he suggested to me, "How about becoming a Maritime Agent, overseeing the loading of ships?"

I stared at him, so surprised I must have looked stupid. Respectfully, I replied, "I don't know anything about maritime operations. Don't you have something else? I just finished a half-decade as an aviator. It's all I know. Boats are something different."

"Yes, I know. But, hey, Big Guy, let your airplanes go. You're not going to make a career there. Listen to me for a bit:

---

* *pastis*: licorice liqueur, very strong, served with water, typical of the Provence region

CHAPTER 16 *Back in France, & Surprise...* 169

You have a Commerce Diploma since you passed your test after three years at Choisy-le-Roi in Paris, and you studied Engineering at the Breguet School. This is all I need to justify hiring you. I'll send you to the city of Marseille for training as a Maritime Agent. One of my branches is linked to a business which loads and unloads cargo, and the director of this business is a good friend. He'll get you trained in short order so we can get you to Saigon right away. I want to see you work for CoGéCo, a competitor to Maritime Freight Forwarders. You'll learn how to supervise dockhands in stowing cargo aboard, then taking it off.

You'll need to know where to place loads both onboard and in warehouses. You'll learn some maritime Law. You'll figure out how to work with the captains, known for being cranky! Above all, your mission will be to load correctly, unload correctly, but always as quickly as possible. Since I know you, Big Guy, I'm sure you'll devour this material in three or four months. You're very capable. You will succeed. So what do you think?"

"Whoa-up," I answered. "You just surpassed the speed of any airplane I ever piloted."

One final point: my uncle let me in on the fact that his associate in Saigon, Director of CoGéCo ("Commerce + *Gérance* (Management) in the Colonies" Company), Mr. de Ligondès, needed a Shipping Agent almost immediately since he wanted to get his ships moving. "If I talk to him about you during your training, he'll be patient until you can fill his position."

Needless to say, as for me it was a "yes" on the spot. As for my future married bliss it would be necessary to talk it over with my wife. I asked my uncle please to wait just a few days for an answer. "I'd like to run it by my parents, and Vera. She just finished her Nursing studies. She'll be here next week to meet my folks."

"Alright," my uncle answered. "As soon as I have your 'ok' I'll send a letter to Marseille. I have another friend that I'll ask to find you a little apartment near the docks. You'll want lodging near your training."

I consulted my father, since his knowledge as a lawyer would give me a valuable opinion on this offer. He would, I hoped, talk over aspects of this kind of position which could prove advantageous or profitable.

Papa thought it was a great idea, especially to think I'd be in Saigon with my uncle, and to think this position might carry with it a promising future. As for my wife, her desire was simply to be with me, no matter where, with her husband whom she hadn't seen for so long. We were still at the honeymoon phase, and my dear wife was learning very nicely how to deal with the French.

One day I politely told her that I wanted to change her first name, which was "Vera." She asked why. I said, "Do you know what *verrat** means in French?" The poor girl was shocked when I revealed the correlation of her name to the pig family.

"Oh my God, what will the French think of me every time I get introduced?"

Would she really change her first name that she'd had since birth, chosen by her mother? Talking it over, with her approval, we decided on the name "Viviane" or "Viane" for short. She liked this name, and when in England she'd still go by "Vera", or "Lottie" as her mother was accustomed to calling her.

My Training in Marseille as Maritime Agent

We packed our bags, ready to jump aboard the train at a moment's notice. We only had to wait one week. Before leaving I was interviewed by the director of CoGéCo who was based in Paris. The branch office in the city of Marseille, on the French Riviera, was called Michel Company, Maritime Agents and Brokers.

It would be in Marseille, then, that I'd get my training, and Uncle Leon had already seen to everything. I received preliminary info in a letter from Mr. Michel, confirming that my arrival in Marseille was expected. He had put me under the supervision of Mr. Bourgerel who was to undertake my training in a rigorous

---

* *verrat*, pronounce veh-RAHH: breeding male of the pig; boar

way. Mr. Michel said I had to pay the way for my wife from Paris to Marseille as well as from Marseille to Saigon after training. Luckily I was able to get a loan from C.C.N.E.O. (*Companie de Commerce Naval de l'Extrême Orient*, hereafter "Maritime Commerce Company of the Far East") in Saigon, which covered her travel costs.

In Marseille we got a hotel room right by the docks. It didn't take long for me to get used to their hours: up early, down to the docks with the workers, familiarizing myself with cranes and platforms and getting to know "the ropes." The important thing aside from these mechanical things was to communicate effectively with dockhands, becoming their colleague rather than a boss. I had plenty of contact with ship captains and their crews, since it was the captains who had to get the cargo manifests from me. With the captain I'd have to discuss the conditions of transporting the cargo, as well as its stowage or warehousing, and there were papers to sign with him when I was sure the cargo had been stowed in accordance with shipping regulations.

Days were long and it was exhausting work, especially since I had to do accounting in the evenings. Sleep had to wait until I did my reading on maritime Law, and much of the terminology threw me. Food was still government-controlled, but I just needed to find a moment to eat!

Sunday was my only day off. My wife and I loved to go to the movies, or we would go out to a café or to a bar for dancing. Near the historic old port of Marseille we enjoyed *la Canebière*, an elegant promenade. Mondays came too quickly, but I got back to it. Since I was required to familiarize myself with the body of unresolved conflicts, I had the help of an aid who knew more about this than I did. With certain shipping problems I was very capable at finding solutions, but those contracts in the arena of "War Shipping" required some deep reading.

Two months flew by. They congratulated me for taking in the whole program very quickly. As planned, this got me the position in Saigon of Maritime Agent, having been certified by the

Maritime Commission of the Far East. I needed to get ready for the job duties which lay ahead, and I had one month left in which to do it. In the meantime I received a letter confirming my contract with Monsieur Henri de Ligondès. This letter listed my responsibilities for a three year stint with Maritime Commerce Company of the Far East, taking into account certain pay increases and a bonus of five thousand francs, the equivalent of four months' pay!

Training to be a Shipping Agent,
city of Marseille, France: 1946

War Pilot Memoirs: A Mirror on 1939

CHAPTER 17

A Precious Soul enters our World

1946 Sees Me back in Indochina

After a long and tiring sea voyage, twenty-eight days on the *SS André Lebon* of Maritime Freight Forwarders, our competitor, my wife and I finally arrived in Saigon. It was Aunt Nini and her husband Joseph Gott who greeted us. They'd offered us temporary accommodations in their sumptuous Saigon property, 230-F rue Pellerin. We were welcomed with very big fanfare: dinner was more a banquet, with all those native Indochinese dishes which I loved so much. *Bâboum*, for example, is a dish served cold made from vermicelli of short grain rice, cucumber and tomato cubes, plus little pieces of beef, all marinated in *nioc-mam*, that fish brine sauce. Yum.

The whole family was there, and for the first time I met some of my cousins, kids of my mom's brother Auguste Châtel. The maiden name of Aunt Betty, Aunt Nini and my *Maman*, three sisters, was Châtel.

Emotionally I was enraptured by this atmosphere. I had left Indochina in 1933 at age 11, yet now I managed to find everything right where it belonged. The exotic fragrance of familiar flowers was lifted by the breeze. My favorite tree was the banyan, budding with all those red blossoms. I noticed a memorable and familiar physiognomy of the servants, aged though they were.

They all lived in a little house in the "park" alongside the main house; it was to the left of the property as you entered. Farther in you had a garage for the cars plus the gardener's house, his wife being a household employee. The cook, plus his wife who served us at the table, were also part of this big family, still there just like twenty years ago, but with kids of their own now. In the colonial lifestyle it was expected that we celebrate and honor old traditions. Everybody was happy. We were celebrating my return and my new career, but moreover we were celebrating one particularly happy event in our future. Viviane was pregnant and we anticipated at any time the welcoming of a new soul.

It was monsoon season. Viviane, uprooted from her English climate, was really suffering from this humid heat. The air was so heavy. It was the 30th of August, 1947, at one o'clock in the morning when she experienced her first contractions and we figured childbirth was imminent. I took Viviane to Saint Paul Clinic where our beautiful daughter Christiane first saw the light of the world. All went well, both for mother and daughter. Oo-la-la, once again we were obligated to celebrate!

In keeping with Drabier family tradition, it was customary to have a nanny the way I'd had a Chinese nanny. My former nurse-nanny Assam was too old to take care of Christiane, so she sent her daughter Amouïe from Hong Kong, who arrived just two weeks after Christiane's birth. It was the pinnacle of joy for me when my mother came all the way from France just to hug her first grandbaby. I found the means to buy my first automobile in which I met *Maman* at the airport. It was a Citroën: convertible and front wheel drive.

The Maritime Commerce Company of the Far East, and Saigon's Upper Crust

Performing my duties, at first, meant working beneath the curious eyes of management. They all were wondering if I'd make it. There was a good reason: they had told me that upon my arrival all the files and such would be ready for me. Dang-it, this was just not the case.

CHAPTER 17 *A Precious Soul enters our World*

At my disposal was a nice little secretary, a Chinaman named Lee-Hong. One day I asked him where I was supposed to find these papers. With an embarrassed air about him, he looked at me. Then we proceeded to a certain door, which, with difficulty, he managed to open. Upon this door, haphazardly attached, was the sign "*Dossiers maritimes*" for "Maritime Documents." Lee-Hong had to drip some oil into the hinges and put his little shoulders to work just to get us in. A nauseating odor of dampness came out of the room; it would almost suffocate you. There were spider webs all over the place. We got some light in there and I could see shelves holding about thirty file boxes on which the writing was so obliterated by dust you couldn't even read it. I tried blowing off some dust, which only created clouds in the already bad air and made me cough violently. Not at all happy with the situation, yet controlling my dismay, I said to Lee-Hong, "How is it that these weren't cleaned up before my arrival?" In truth I was on the brink of manifesting my anger.

A bit intimidated, Lee backed up. With a certain lack of assertiveness in his voice, he said, "Monsieur, I am sorry. It was only minutes ago that I got the key to this room for the first time."

I knew it wasn't his fault, so I patted him on the shoulder, saying, "Ok, let's get to work. Clean this up for me."

I didn't want to start off looking as though I was ticked off at management, so just to calm myself down I headed for the port where I knew a bar in the big café-restaurant. There I got to meet all kinds of people, and they all had important positions. We exchanged business cards. I had the honor of meeting someone who would become crucial in my life: Mr. Boubal, Chief Commissioner of the Saigon Police. We hit it off right away. He said to me, "I know your father really well. I even sent many a Chinese client to his office." A few days later he invited me to the sports center where all of upper-crust Saigon got together in the evening after work, just about 6pm when the heat of the day subsided and was replaced by a faint but refreshing little breeze. This sports center was huge with its tennis courts, swimming pools, bar, restaurant, a room for playing bridge, one for billiards and one for the infamous roulette wheel. All the members of my side of the family could at times be found there. My cousin Gisou, who loved to swim, was a real "fish" in their pool.

After only a month at the company I brought in a ship all by myself: a twenty-five thousand ton freighter of Ho Hong Steamship Company, a Chinese firm. I was so proud, especially when I'd finished with no disasters. Another month went by, and I brought in a forty-five thousand ton freighter belonging to Blue Funnel, a company based in Great Britain, with passengers onboard who were mainly British. Oh, what work!

Luckily my little secretary knew more about it all than I did. He was of infinite value, especially as concerned the passengers. Then, too, there was Mr. Marty, the director of the department overseeing food both for passengers and for crew: his position was called *Shipchandler*. I learned he had been the one who'd handled the Shipping Department before me, but he preferred restocking the foodstuffs. Later I would learn how much more profitable this was for him, but, for now, it was just a good thing that he had changed jobs to open this one up for me.

Ship-stocking Manager: *Shipchandler*

By 1949 I had gained the respect of management. Just about every month I'd bring in one or two ships of sixty-five thousand tons. These came from, among others, an American firm, the Stan Line. My duties within my department were becoming more and more extensive, so much so that I now had another secretary and an accountant. By the same token I was getting more time off, time I spent with my wife and my one-and-a-half year old daughter Christiane.

We thanked Aunt Nini for having helped so much by giving us lodging. We decided to move into a comfortable house with a big yard on Boulevard Charner. In our new household we had a cook, the cook's wife who took care of housekeeping, plus Christiane's nanny Amouïe. Our nanny was gifted with sewing talents so she fabricated pretty little dresses for my daughter.

CHAPTER 17 *A Precious Soul enters our World*

Our circle of friends grew: the Rosenfeldts, he being a real estate manager and loan officer, the Savaris, he being an import-export specialist. Just about every weekend, one of the couples, we included, would invite the others over. One thing which must be said about colonial life: everything got done with pomp and circumstance. When couples got invited over, they would bring their servants with them, and the servants helped serve there where one had been invited. The servants of the hosting home and those of the invitees got all gussied up in white, but with black turbans on their heads. And thus went our lives in those years 1948 to 1949. Of course I had known such a lifestyle before World War II with my parents. Daily life *à la colonie* was generally sumptuous, since both elegance and etiquette were in force. This environment disappeared with the war of the Vietminh. The Vietcong, their military faction, ended up chasing us off, to put it mildly, as they abolished this colonial era.

*   *   *

I experienced great success as a maritime agent. From 1947 to 1950 I earned a fortune and I invested my proceeds into various projects. I acquired a rubber plantation which stretched over four miles in width and over five miles in length. It was in the "red soil" country near the three borders of Annam (encompassing modern day North and South Vietnam), Cambodia and my southern homeland of *Cochinchine*. For this project I needed an airplane, so I chose a model equipped for tourism: a Nord 1000, four-seater. I had to get a civilian license, but since I had my certification as a military pilot, switching over was pretty easy.

Soon I was donned with a new function by the company: I got the job of *Shipchandler*, the position held by Mr. Marty when I had arrived. This Marty often found himself fighting with the *compradors*, the food buyers. To eliminate the problem, the company simply offered him another post.

In this new work domain, I learned quickly enough what the expression "under the table" really means. The amounts involved came to five or six times my salary! When the *shipchandler* had to buy some five or ten tons of food with which to stock the ship (fish, meat, rice, vegetables, wines), he obtained it by negotiating with the *compradors*, who generally fought tooth and nail among themselves to obtain a part of the order. Once the lowest bid was identified, the order got placed. At my disposal there were five permanently established *compradors*, so my supplemental profit was simply a foregone conclusion.

Whenever a big meat order came in, the ship's butcher had to trim all the fat, so I was blessed with tons of beef fat on my hands. You see, by maritime law I was the only beneficiary of this beef fat, which I could do with as I pleased. In Saigon, I knew a local soap manufacturer who paid me a good price for it, then I augmented my net worth by investing the income.

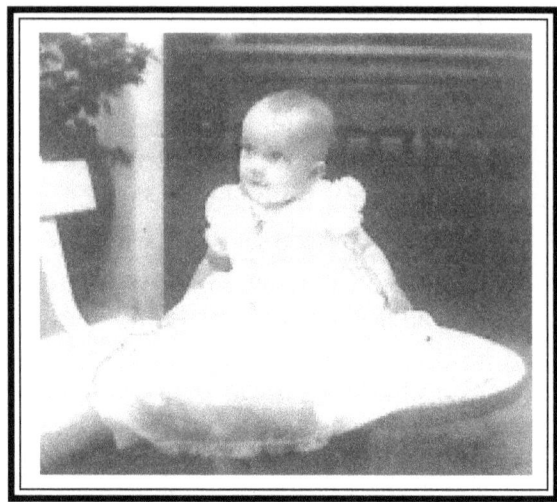

The christening of my daughter Christiane

War Pilot Memoirs: A Mirror on 1939

CHAPTER 18

Curare, Cobras, and Tiger Cubs

Life in Saigon was going downhill fast; there were violent assaults every day. The Nationalist Organization of the Vietminh wanted its independence from the French, so life got pretty risky, especially in business. The Vietminh monopolized more and more to drive prices up, and you didn't know from one day to the next with whom you were dealing. Rather than the Vietminh, I preferred doing business with the Chinese. Since these Chinese were quite rich, they themselves became targets of the Vietcong, the military arm of the Vietminh.

France's Vietnam War

France had already started to battle the Vietminh nationalists, so we unfortunate civilians were caught in the middle of perilous circumstances. We were surrounded by people we did not trust anymore, and you got yourself shot at, just for a "yes" or a "no." The police force was becoming so very powerless, to the point that one day the Army simply declared that everyone was on his own. The Army was too busy warring in jungles and rice patties, so we took to arming ourselves in a very serious way. Even so, I knew a few unspoiled places which were not too dangerous.

Christiane, my precious fragile flower, was christened on

Wednesday the 11th of August, 1948, in the same Saigon church where I'd had my First Communion at about the age of nine. I used to love going out in public with my daughter. I was proud of my little family, so Viviane, Christiane and I often went to the Botanical Gardens of Saigon. They had a great restaurant there, musicians were playing on the bandstands, and this part of town was still protected by armed Military Police. I'd take the family out in that Citroën of mine, and like every kid I've ever known, Christiane adored going for a ride in "the car." This little two-year-old understood several languages: English from her mom, French from me and my family, Chinese from her nanny and finally Indochinese since she was always in the company of local servants.

Notwithstanding the shaky political climate, I sometimes got the chance to go hunting in the higher elevations of what later was called South Vietnam, up there near my rubber plantation and my uncle's. His was much bigger than mine, yet they were side by side. These plantations were near Laos and Cambodia.

My uncle and I hunted tigers. On one occasion, unintentionally, my uncle killed a female tiger and then found some tiger cubs close by. He couldn't leave them, so he and his group carried them back. His wife, my Aunt Betty, was plenty zealous in the way she looked after them, and she took great pleasure in playing with her miniature Wild Kingdom.

CAMBODIA – Tiger Hunting – Story of the Cobra

Prior to 1933, at my school there in Indochina, I'd been in the same class with the cousin of Prince Sianouk of Cambodia. He went by "Boulok", and completely by accident we bumped into each other, so he invited me to go hunting on the Royal Game Preserve! This area hadn't yet been occupied by Vietcong. This kind of hunt is fabulous, a real safari. You go out for ten days, weather permitting; you cannot trail tigers in the rain, because they always duck in and take cover. We would be traveling by elephant-back with our guides leading the way. We would transport much equipment since we'd be camping in the jungle.

CHAPTER 18 *Curare, Cobras, and Tiger Cubs*

I was ecstatic to be invited, so I got busy setting myself up with porters and a guide. Guides were daring, armed to the teeth "just in case"; they protected us. All the guides and porters were indigenous, of the Moï tribe, somewhat primitive but extremely devoted. They all came armed with bows they'd fabricated and they used arrows which were poison-tipped with curare. This vegetable substance paralyses human muscles, yet we could see it all around us dripping from the trees. The sap which these trees secrete is curare. Truth be told, I didn't feel any too confident when these Moïs were around me with their arrows, so I constantly sidestepped to avoid a scratch from a poisoned tip. A prick would be the equivalent of a snakebite, maybe not fatal but certainly causing paralysis.

Those of the Moï tribe lived in little villages of a hundred people, one of which comprised the workers on my rubber plantation. Their houses, or rather their huts, were built on stilts. These elevated huts gave them a feeling of security regarding serpents and wild animals that might attack them while the Moïs slept. They possessed a deep knowledge of the jungle and its plants, many of which they gathered for medicinal use.

*   *   *

So off we went: I met up with Boulok, this being his family name because in Cambodia it was rare to hear people use their first names, even though they sometimes got nicknames. He had a big group of guides and porters who were better provisioned than my team, given his social standing as royalty. His guards were armed with guns.

The first two days we made progress deep into the jungle. At a certain point we had to leave the three elephants since the jungle got too thick. They would be escorted back by one of the indigenous tribesmen of our team. We continued our trek afoot. Still nothing, no tigers! The fourth day we arrived at a little cabaña, built and furnished expressly for hunters. It was a true Mecca both as shelter and as a place to rest: food and potable water, hammocks for sleeping, plus just being a safe haven. No electricity, though, so we used petroleum lamps for light.

The Cobra

We walked up. Boulok announced we should spend the night here and offer ourselves a decent meal instead of the infernal canned sardines and sausages. A good soup was boiling and filled the air with its aroma as we seated ourselves at a big round table. The guides and a few other chosen, fortunate ones joined the upper class at this table. There was Boulok, his bodyguards, I, my guide; there were six or eight of us all told. The heat was stifling. Above the table was a big *panka*. This was a screen suspended from the ceiling, fabricated out of bamboo cane and fronds, measuring about two yards long by one yard wide. It was operated by long ropes which, about five or six yards away from the table, descended to the floor. Pulling on these ropes did create a very refreshing breeze, and we were swimming in our own sweat.

It was time to eat, so Boulok told one of his porters to take the rope and give us a little air movement. Our dear porter crouched down in the corner and started pulling on the rope to operate the *panka*. Abruptly an unidentified mass fell onto the middle of the table! This made everybody jump. It was a cobra of impressive size that had set up housekeeping atop the *panka*, altogether comfortable. Suddenly disturbed by its motion, which he didn't appreciate even a bit, here he was, hissing and puffing up and looking at us, all of which was to say, "Look out. I'm on the attack!" We were all glued to our seats.

Boulok said very calmly, "All of you, bury your head and shoulders at the level of the tabletop, and do it smoothly!" He said to his bodyguard, equipped with a big jungle knife called a *coupe-coupe* or a *yatagan*, "Gently, gently sneak behind that snake." Cobras don't see what's happening behind them, so we all figured out the plan. The cobra, still hissing, seemed to fixate on something in front of him, so he didn't turn anymore. Taking advantage of momentary hesitation on the part of the cobra, the guard, now directly behind… wham! With one swift, precise blow, the guard decapitated the cobra with his *yatagan*.

Wow! That snake squirmed as he jumped into the air, contorting in every direction with a flailing motion that had us all sprinkled with his blood. We jumped out of our chairs instinctively. I had lost my appetite; so had the rest.

My Tiger

The next day our guides told us they were on the trail of a tiger. We needed to check the wind direction because when a tiger knows the chase is on, he develops a sixth sense and his cunning combines with uncanny wariness. The hunter can become the hunted, and the wind direction is a determining factor. All the while we talked about the previous evening, which we were beginning to tell jokes about. The big laugh was the look on our faces and our physiognomy, those of us who had been sitting around that table, in our moment of anguish. What an adventure! Happy we were to have the Moï guides with us.

Another surprise awaited us. We were heading for a waterfall that we had seen from afar. There was a light breeze that morning which felt so refreshing on our sweaty backs. We were following our guides' signals, walking slowly, rifles at the ready. In that immense forest there was that special kind of silence interrupted only by outcries from birds. All around us we had nothing but giant trees from which vines were hanging. Of a sudden, my guide, who was just three steps ahead of me, froze. Boulok was fifteen feet in front of him, stopped under a tree. Boulok was walking point, on the lookout where you had to turn your head constantly from left to right. On my left stood one of Boulok's bodyguards, rifle to his shoulder preparing to fire!

All at once like a bolt of lightning a mass descended from the tree, which was about thirty feet tall. This mass was going to attack Boulok. Bang, bang, bang! Three shots rang out at the same time: from the bodyguard, from my guide and from me. These killed the tiger on the spot, the tiger that was about to kill the prince, and it fell at the feet of Boulok. We all stood there with our mouths gaping open.

The whole occurrence seemed surprising, and with good reason, because it is rare to find tigers hiding out on tree limbs. This tree was particularly low-hanging, with limbs which paralleled the ground. With dismay we discovered this tiger to be a female, regrettable since we serious hunters always tried to avoid killing tigresses. Given the circumstances, this time had been unavoidable. We were still in the process of looking over this inert mass when, from behind the tree, two little babies appeared, meowing, stumbling along the jungle floor toward their lifeless mother. I myself could not help feeling responsible. We scooped the little ones up in our arms, as they were only about two weeks old. Boulok regained his composure, walked toward us, took one of the little ones and said to me, "Jacques, thank you for your promptness. I owe you my life. Here, take one of the little ones in remembrance of this. May he become your friend, and you will be his mommy. I'll take the other one as a symbol of recognition for his true mother, who was killed out of necessity." That tigress really was a beauty.

The Moï tribesmen trimmed up some bamboo to make two little cages and the porters were able to carry them, slung on a long piece of bamboo, on their shoulders. I named my little tiger "Boulok" in remembrance of that day and of my friend, but I asked permission first. Boulok, the prince's cousin, seemed very proud of the idea, as he said to me, smiling, "I hope it's a boy."

"*Eh bien oui,*" I confirmed. "Yes, it's a boy."

After such an emotional encounter we made a beeline for the village. We carried along the tigress's carcass, and upon our arrival the tribe took to skinning it. That beautiful hide would be the trophy of Boulok, the prince's cousin. The tribe would have the meat, which by the way is very tasty. It was certainly their turn to have some compensation. At the Moï village I had a talk with the chief, letting him know that my little cub would be staying at the village. The chief would be responsible for feeding

CHAPTER 18 *Curare, Cobras, and Tiger Cubs* 185

him, yet being very careful not to let him get a taste for raw meat. They were to let him run free, allowing him to interact with the chickens and the pigs.

My little tiger Boulok got big very fast, but he was a docile and affectionate playmate to anyone. Because I now had an airplane, I was able to visit the plantation several times a month, so I visited my tiger at the same time. It was just like playing with a big pussycat, and I was jealous of his liberty as I shared it with him. I took him to the lake where we bathed together. It took me aback each time I saw his increase in size. To look at him, one could imagine a ferocious beast, but this tiger possessed an almost human kindness.

Many years later, when the movie <u>Born Free</u> came out, oh how I found it impossible not to dream about my tiger. This movie, produced in the 1960s, was a story identical to Boulok's. A couple had adopted a little lion and in growing up he became their pal, following them everywhere, playing with them. Today I cannot resist tracing a parallel.

The timeline of Boulok was 1948, and in a matter of months my tiger grew to an imposing size and strength; you'd have even called him immense. I still played with him, but when he put his paws on my shoulders his weight did, half the time, knock me over backwards. But Boulok loved playing with me, just like a favorite toy. I was surprised when the tribal chief shared with me how, after several days wandering in the jungle, Boulok would come right back to home as if nothing had happened. With his oversized kitten-paw he'd push a little piglet along the trail, but he'd do it with such finesse that the piglet never knew the difference.

One day Uncle Leon came with me, and he too marveled at such an immense beast that was so gentle and pretty. My uncle let me know that he had been approached by one of his friends, Monsieur Legrand, director of the Conservation and Humane Society. My uncle said, "This director is aware of your little secret. He's worried that Boulok now circulates in the jungle, going any which way." My uncle pointed out to me that on these plantations there were men who raised cattle, and these cows attracted tigers from the jungle. Feeding on cattle sometimes, if tigers got too close the farmers had the right to shoot them. If perchance Boulok were to stray into fields bordering on these cattle pastures, then the farmers would be hard pressed to know the difference.

This concerned me since I didn't want a bad event of any nature to befall my Boulok. Since Monsieur Legrand was the most knowledgeable, we needed to take his advice. We needed to let Boulok loose in the forest, so my uncle and I took him a good seventy miles north of the village, into the brush country far from civilization, so he wouldn't risk getting killed. I left him there, but my heart was very heavy.

Two weeks later our Boulok had made his way back to the village, but he was all scratched up and he had lost weight. I bet he hadn't been able to find food. We needed a new approach. If we took him farther away, say a few hundred miles, well, I don't think he'd have survived. He did not know how to hunt to feed himself. Even other tigers might have climbed on him and killed him, so we ruled out this option. Uncle Leon told me he had spoken with his friend the director of the Saigon Zoo. This was a huge zoo, and in the area for jungle animals they had a section for caged tigers. When all was said and done, this seemed the best option. We constructed a special cage for Boulok and transported him via truck to Saigon. This expedition took two weeks, and just to think how my airplane could do it in 45 minutes. My little plane could not carry such a cage, and my tiger had gotten too heavy.

Thus concludes the destiny of my tiger, Boulok. For him, a loss of liberty, and for me a loss of the dream to share liberty with him. At least he was alive.

* * *

CHAPTER 18 *Curare, Cobras, and Tiger Cubs*

Meanwhile the situation in Indochina was deteriorating rapidly. There were more and more deadly assaults, right out in public. We felt no more security in any method of transit. At all times I kept a case of grenades which I had managed to acquire under the seat of my Jeep, right along with a Thompson machinegun. On my person, tucked under my left arm, I always had a .38 caliber Smith and Wesson revolver. Often enough I carried a Colt .45 caliber on my right hip too! Deplorable as it was to play Rambo this way, it had simply become a necessity. Don't even mention the police who could not make their own indigenous population feel safe. We had official permission to carry weapons, so carry weapons we did. As the police officer might have said, "Every man for himself."

War Pilot Memoirs: A Mirror on 1939

CHAPTER 19

The Las Vegas of the Orient

June, 1950. The Vietcong were winning on every front. I had almost completed my contract with the Company, so I wanted to focus on my rubber plantation; selling fifty-pound blocks of rubber sap was going to take some effort. I used to scoot back and forth by airplane to have a look-see at parts of the plantation which had not yet been worked, where the trees had not yet been tapped. I actually had to buy extra trucks just to get all the materials transported. My biggest buyers were Chinese, and one of them was located in the city of Cholon, about twelve miles north of Saigon, so that particular day I took off by Jeep, still well armed, just in case. I had to traverse a dangerous part of the jungle, the danger coming from the Vietcong. The dirt road had been washed away somewhat by monsoons. Along the ditches and at the edge of the jungle growth, the vegetation could be very dense. Because there was no other road for getting around this particular section of jungle, off I went.

The Vietcong guerrillas liked this corner of the jungle and camouflaged themselves in the brush. They'd carry out an attack, a surprise ambush, then scurry away, all so quick that you didn't have time to pick your nose or figure out what was up. There I was, passing through this way by lack of alternative, and

I was not very long on confidence. I was being extra careful. As I drove into perhaps the densest vegetation, I got a whiff of gunpowder! I told myself that there'd been some dirty business here, and not long ago. I had two choices: roll through at high speed, or retrace my path and get the hell out of there. I paused to think. What to do? No matter what, I had to make a quick decision. I said to myself, "They did their dirty work, so are they gone?" Night had fallen, which made my job even tougher. Hoo-rah, here I went. I decided to move on, pressing my accelerator to the floor.

Just after gunning my Jeep up to full speed, I saw, way up ahead on my left, two beams of light which strangely pointed up to the sky at a 45 degree angle. No noise, and these light beams were stationary. This concerned me a bit. What the devil could it be? Cautious as a soldier manning the point, I approached the place where the lights were. The light source was buried in the brush, and I could not figure out what it was. I just had to stop, but, whoa, surely this was a trap! I stood up in the Jeep after chambering a round in my machinegun, and there were two grenades clipped to my belt. I spat out a few rounds in circles around me, ready for battle if anyone were there. Nothing moved. I hopped down from the Jeep, weapon in hand, still on the lookout. I forced my way into the brush where the lights were shining. Right away I saw an American-made car turned upside down in the ditch, all four wheels in the air, the headlights still on. These were the streams of light I'd seen in the sky. I could tell that the attack had happened immediately prior to my arrival, and it had been one infernal attack.

Turning to go back to my Jeep, I heard moaning and unarticulated pleas coming from over there. I looked closer, trying to see where these moans were coming from. I found a Chinese man near the car. He was all bloody and there was blood all around him to boot. What a horrible sight: his throat was slit open. He was wearing a dress suit, a white one made of silk, of the "short-skin" so popular then for the wealthy Chinese. This

CHAPTER 19 *The Las Vegas of the Orient*

outfit he was wearing was one pricy piece of work, making me think this guy must be a big wig. Moreover, a Cadillac was not a common car in this part of the world.

Rich or poor, I could not abandon this guy in the brush to die. It took some doing, but I got him into my Jeep. This poor wretch was not going to see the light of even one more day, but the only humane thing to do was to try to save him. The best way I could help was to go on to Cholon where there was a hospital. It was the closest one anyway. Once in the Emergency Room, I told them what had transpired, leaving my name and address. I went on my way, convinced that this poor guy would not survive.

*   *   *

Given the war with the Vietcong, which was rising in fervor, it was less and less often that ships called on our port. You could easily see this in our paperwork. Thus my sales to the soap manufacturer were suffering. I sold less and less animal fat for soap, and for margarine which was a similar sideline. Margarine has been around since the late 1800s and in the early days it did indeed contain animal bi-products.

No more ships, no more grease, so my commissions were reduced to nil. For this and other reasons I asked that the contract, for my duties as Maritime Agent, be terminated at the first opportunity. My superiors sympathized and they were indulgent as they encouraged me to take a few months "on the slow." They did not penalize me for cutting off my contract, given the circumstances, that is to say a basic state of civil war. My profit center, then, became my plantation.

A rubber plantation, staffed with Moï tribesmen, was a marvel to behold. Raw rubber sap, gooey in consistency, flowed slowly into a drinking glass sized container on each tree, and the tribesmen gathered this milky-white substance into "toocks", terra cotta or ceramic containers they carried on their backs. At our central storage facility, which we called the "hangar", a machine stirred it up with a liquefying agent. This produced yellowish white cubes in a mold which had ejection-hinges. These cubes, eighteen inches or more in height, were the product to be sold.

I got a big order from Australia for my raw rubber sap. They sent fifty percent payment in advance on an order for fifty tons of product! This huge sum arrived by international check, which had to be validated by the Indochinese *Banque Générale*, the only bank authorized to make such an international transfer.

Surprise at the Indochinese Bank

As I walked into the bank in Saigon, I couldn't help but notice what a truly impressive building it was. Everything was marble, on the outside as well as the inside. There were huge columns in front of the entranceway, and the walls were adorned with fine paintings. Statues and furniture alike were examples of oriental art of the highest quality, and a plush carpet covered the floor. I headed for the waiting area where several others were already waiting. A *huissier* [pronounce hweess-ee-AY], the man who announced to the administrators which clients were waiting, approached. I gave him my calling card. I needed to wait, since there were five other people sitting there already. This *huissier* had an air of worth and dignity, all dressed up in his fine business attire, with a silver chain across his vest. It was he who had access to the *Directeur Général*, the Bank Manager. One had to wait one's turn patiently, so, prim and proper, I seated myself for the duration of time it might require.

I had been sitting a sum total of three minutes when the *huissier* came straight toward me and said, "Monsieur Drabier, will you please follow me?" I showed a little hesitation as I looked him in the eye and gesticulated my concern for the other clients. Without blinking, he insisted with a smile, graciously bent forward in a bow, and then showed me to a door which he opened in saying, "Monsieur Sou-Tin-Saô is expecting you, monsieur." He motioned me to advance, I entered, and the door closed behind me.

Oops, I just about tripped, the carpet was so thick. There was very little light in this grand hall; for me it was a bit too dark. I had no clue what was going on. The room was huge. I saw a glorious wooden desk surrounded by marble columns and alongside the desk a shadow that was standing upright. I wondered to myself: why so dark in this office? I couldn't even make out the physiognomy of that person in the dark. I walked forward ever so carefully, a bit confused, not knowing what to think.

Suddenly every light in the room came on, and I saw before me a well-dressed Chinese gentleman. He was wearing white Chinese silk, short-skin fabric. He was smiling at me as he said, with a voice full and strong, "I did not know that Mr. Drabier, my lawyer, had a son." He came over to shake my hand and said, "It is my great privilege and an honor to meet you, for I owe you my life." I was dumbfounded, my eyes aghast, as he undid his white silk scarf, uncovering his throat where there was a large and fresh scar, even with the marks left by sutures. He said, "I'm the man in the brush in that jungle, with my throat cut, after the Vietcong attack."

Boy, was I ever shaken up! I stared at him as if I were seeing a phantom. He continued, "They did good work at the hospital, but the fact I'm alive today is due to you, and the six hours of surgery they performed. You see, if you hadn't taken me in, I never would have seen another sunrise. I'm indebted to you for the rest of my days, as I am indebted to your family also." He took my check without even looking at it, saying, "Just see my secretary, who'll take care of this right away. Then, dear sir, do me the honor of bringing your wife when you come to my home tomorrow, for we have a great deal to talk about. I'll present the two of you to my sizeable family." After I'd accepted his invitation, he gave me a hug with both arms. My head was still spinning, as I was having trouble getting over this surprise.

*   *   *

The next day, babysitting and miscellaneous details arranged, we honored his invitation. The estate of Monsieur Sou-Tin-Saô was immense. Along one side was a manmade lake filled with water lilies and lotus plants. Gardeners were working here and there and egrets promenaded in the lake. Little walkways lined with banyan trees were everywhere. Some peacocks were strutting around and giving their piercing cry.

We arrived in my car, pulling up in front of the veranda's six columns. Right away, two nicely dressed servants opened our car doors and directed us toward the door of the house where an elegant lady wearing a silk dress cut in a Chinese style, with vibrant colors and with gold or silver inlay, stood next to Monsieur Sou-Tin-Saô. He was dressed in an oriental suit of the style very popular among businessmen of rank. We were impressed by the sumptuousness of the surroundings. There were many, many servants. We were led to an enormous receiving room, very modern, with a European motif, and furnished in very good taste. There were several ceramic vases from three all the way to six feet in height in the style of the Ming Dynasty, early 1400s. In this receiving room there stood eight nice tall girls aged from 18 to 25 years. All were his daughters, and they were very pretty and elegant. They spoke fluent French, yet addressed my wife Viviane in English. One of them spoke Russian, Japanese and German. It was easy to see that his daughters had studied well, and in schools of good standing.

The evening meal was an epicurean delight, an assortment of little servings of wonderfully prepared foods. Our host had his own personal orchestra comprised of European musicians playing French and American melodies. We even danced. Out of the corner of my eye I was watching my wife who was both worried and intimidated. Our host had invited Viane to dance, but since I knew her to be good on her feet, this didn't concern me. What can I say? The evening was like a story out of <u>The Arabian Nights</u>.

Monsieur Sou-Tin-Saô had three wives, which goes to explain all those daughters, and he had sons too. The Buddhist religion legally allowed for marrying several women. China in those days was better off, as regards social stability, until its government years later put an end to polygamy.

CHAPTER 19 *The Las Vegas of the Orient*

Buddhism was different from Islam in this regard. Islamic tradition authorized men to claim superiority over women, possessions that had to cover themselves from head to toe. In China's tradition of Buddhism, granted a woman had only one husband, yet a woman was to be respected. The husband was allowed to take on several wives, but he was required to have financial means to do so, just as he was required to respect their value as individuals. In a powerful way, by customs and morals, this high Chinese society was codified, or so I was told, the first wife being responsible for the social activities of the couple. The second wife held primary responsibility for procreating. The third, they told me, would manage the household, including meals and overseeing the servants.

Well, let's get back to this festive evening where I was the guest of honor. At his home there was music, dancing, and glorious food without end, but our host invited me to meet him the next day at the infamous *Café du Commerce* on the street called *rue Catina*. He wanted to talk some kind of business over with me, yet it had been important to him that I know who his family was, and what his background was, before discussing with me his dream, his brainchild: whatever it was he wanted to concoct with my help. I'd learned he came from southern China, born in Fukien, also called Fujian, Province. His forefathers, including his dad, had been very wealthy merchants, so his fortunes were "without horizons." It was rather academic that he accepted a salary for his position as *Directeur Général* at the bank, since his holdings outweighed those of his colleagues a thousand times over.

Several times he had needed the services of my father as a defense attorney, and they had become good friends. Now I was still asking myself what the heck his "dream" might be, but before describing it to you, I'd better cover an important point concerning the nature of doing business with the Chinese in that era. In the city of Cholon there was a large Chinese subpopulation, and, among them, many aristocrats from what we'll call "Old

China." These magnates possessed sizeable fortunes, but theirs was a society which was closed off to French high society. Monsieur Sou-Tin-Saô, very much the modern man as regards European political and business thinking, despised this attitude on the part of the Chinese, because it diminished how much business could get done. It was a brake on the economy.

As he explained it, he had tried several approaches, varying forms of business philosophy, but these had yielded no favorable result. In the city of Cholon there existed what we called *Kimchung* for "the golden bells." It was a gambling establishment controlled by Chinese high-rollers. It had its own security force, both for the gaming rooms and for an area where stage productions were presented, but their weapons were generally concealed to avoid scaring the patrons. All of this was on such a scale as to make Las Vegas look small. (Well, Las Vegas was just getting its start there in the desert.)

The gambling establishment in Cholon was licensed by the French government. Every nine months an auction was held which produced income payable to the state. Thus, at the end of every nine month period, bids were placed, and the group of Chinese businessmen who bid the highest would be managers of this "city of gaming" for the upcoming nine months. There were several groups: the Peking Group, the Shanghai Group, the Fukien Group from the Province of Fujian in China just across the water from Taiwan, the Hong Kong Group and many others.

This particular year, 1948 or 1949, Monsieur Sou-Tin-Saô had bid highest at the auction. He said to me, "Ah, I know that with your help I'll be able to realize my dream!" I was getting very curious, so I listened attentively. Where was he going with this? He continued, "As you know, Monsieur Drabier, the two high societies, French and Chinese, don't get along. They don't even communicate with each other. This creates a very negative situation for business."

I replied, "You're exactly right."

Revealing his secret now, he continued, "As you know, I just

CHAPTER 19 *The Las Vegas of the Orient* 197

became the new manager, having won the *Kimchung* auction. Yes, the two elements of society often go to the Golden Bells for gaming to entertain themselves, but they never mingle to discuss any business. So my idea is to have built, and very rapidly, an expansion of several rooms in the Jaquarero Building. It is eight stories tall. On the terrace I'll be adding a theater for Chinese-European stage productions. This would be open to both sectors of society as an attraction to have businessmen mingle."

"Hum," was my reply as I raised an eyebrow, "you think this will work? It's like invading the domain of a dragon and putting elephants there!"

He smiled. "This will succeed, thanks to you."

I didn't comprehend the connection. So, Monsieur Sou-Tin-Saô, enthusiastic as they come, paused politely, then winked at me as he said, "I'd like you to accept my offer to direct my new project, your title to be Diplomatic Director of Gaming."

Courteously I smiled, but I explained to him that I was still working for the Maritime Commerce Company of the Far East as a *shipchandler*. "The little time I get outside of work I like to spend with my family. I'm very appreciative, and honored by the offer, but I do not see how I could accept."

After another polite pause, he said, "I would not ask for all of your time, but only a few hours of your presence in the evenings. You and your family are already very well known to businessmen here, especially your father who is respected by all these magnates on the Chinese side. You yourself have an honorable reputation which is exemplary, most especially with what you did for me! This is beyond measure. I will pay you for both your time and inconvenience. I'll pay five gold *tahells* per week. A brand new office will be constructed for you on the terrace, within 48 hours. You'll need a secretary, so one of my daughters will serve you in this capacity. You'll choose the one you wish. The girls are all well-qualified in this arena and they'll be proud to help their father."

Wow, my head was starting to swim! How to refuse? It would

certainly be the first time I'd see pay in gold *tahells*. The *tahell* was a rectangular piece of gold about two inches long by an inch wide, as thick as two dozen sheets of paper, made of 24 carat gold. With good liquidity, they were traded at any Chinese bank. One *tahell* was worth a hundred Indochinese piasters, each piaster being worth seventeen French francs, the cost of dinner for two at a restaurant. Just one *tahell*, then, would have paid for one hundred dinners for two!

Monsieur Sou-Tin-Saô was very insistent and begged me to accept. Speaking to me as if to a colleague, he said, "I am sure you'll have good success, and I envision a change in the flow of things, a broadening, a genuine improvement in Franco-Chinese relations. Don't forget, this would only last nine months."

I headed home, still mulling this offer over in my mind, knowing a discussion with my wife was called for. She was all happy and giggly when she greeted me. With unbounded excitement, she said, "Come look at what someone sent me! A uniformed chauffeur brought me this huge bouquet of exotic flowers, and a box covered with red velvet."

All smiles, Viane opened the box very carefully, then pulled out the contents to show me the most elegant jade necklace I've ever seen, and there was a matching bracelet. These were crafted of jade sectioned off with layers of gold. It seemed a gift fit for a queen! Right away I knew where this gift had come from, as well as the reason for it. To myself I was thinking: oh, yes, this Sou-Tin-Saô knows how to lubricate the situation. Playing his most refined philosophical hand, he must have realized that being courteous and generous to my wife would bring me around.

*   *   *

A grand success, this affair, yet I must affirm that adding this new responsibility was a burden. Luckily my shipping duties were coming to an end. Viane voiced a few objections since this took me away from evenings we'd otherwise spend together. She preferred that we go out together to visit friends or enjoy some other kind of high society function.

CHAPTER 19 *The Las Vegas of the Orient*

Since I was the adventurer, this all represented for me a chance to play runaway child. Anyway, I accepted. I do love adventure. I phoned Monsieur Sou-Tin-Saô, ceding acceptance. He didn't waste a minute, urging me to get over to his office right away. "We need 'posthaste' to sign a contract." To myself I thought he feared my backing out.

I understood. Following the established rules of society and of business was indeed important, so I got to his office where I was surprised to find one of his daughters present. She displayed the elegance of a mannequin in the shop of an haut-couturier. Indeed it was a Parisian business-dress she was wearing. She presented herself saying, "My name is Mai-Lingh. I would be very happy to be your secretary."

Monsieur Sou-Tin-Saô told me, "You can ask her questions, and if this one doesn't suit you then you'll query my other daughters."

Right away Mai-Lingh followed up with, "I take dictation. I know all the technical procedures involved in gaming." Smiling ever so graciously, she had already won me over. I didn't go to the trouble of querying her on anything, not wanting to embarrass her, for I knew her pedigree.

Inauguration of the Jaquarero Building

This was quite the ceremony. The Chinese Theater, with characteristic artwork, had comfortable, plush chairs for all the Chinese and European aristocrats. A grandiose orchestra was playing melodies from China and from Europe with equal dexterity. I had personally invited several Saigon businessmen, among them the Vice Consul of Great Britain, the director of Maritime Freight Forwarders, the Chief of Police, the Advocate General of the Department of Justice, and many others. Mai-Lingh surprised us with a piece of Chinese theater, a comedy in which the theme was the integration of the two societies. It was a musical, almost Las Vegas style, and she showed a very refined and delicate sense of humor. All was an impressive success. Monsieur Sou-Tin-Saô, enchanted by a feminine entourage, was happy like a cat lapping up milk. His invitees had an enjoyable evening, and they seemed appreciative.

* * *

Notwithstanding these work evenings I managed to sneak away to the plantation occasionally. Once I was able to take a few days off and fly my wife to Cap Saint Jacques, a cape on the South China Sea coast of *Cochinchine*. Luckily we had my airplane to get away in, because those lousy roads, poorly maintained to start with, were the scene of many an attack. Most roads were literally under Vietcong control, and Saigon itself was getting to be "Assassination Central."

Some of my friends from the tiger hunts were out to eat, in a mixed group, at a well-reputed, open-air restaurant in the city of Cholon. Some little kid threw a grenade which skipped, like a stone on a lake, down a long alley until it came to rest under the table. The explosion wounded many of them seriously. One of the ones hospitalized was Robert Rosenfeldt, a close friend. I went to visit him in the hospital, but unfortunately he died a few days later.

Suicide of the British Vice Consul

The nine months at *Kimchung*, the Golden Bells, went by quickly and uneventfully. Nevertheless, there was one regrettable scenario which I'll never forget. It was a pleasant evening, as was customarily the case. One of my Chinese employees who worked on the terrace level came running up to me, all wide-eyed. He was practically screaming. "*Patron, Patron*, come quick! Mister Bern is drunk. He's walking on the wall around the terrace. He won't listen to anybody, and I'm afraid of trying to grab him."

This wall around the terrace, designed to keep anyone from falling off, had a top surface only ten inches wide, and it was on the eighth floor. I approached with the greatest caution this Mr.

Bern who was wobbling and singing at the top of his lungs. He had his arms stretched out for balance. He would not listen to me, and I found myself perturbed by this. A crowd had gathered below, looking to see what was going to transpire, and the crowd perturbed me too since it was too noisy. I was about three feet away, only three feet, so I thought to myself: Maybe I can grab his legs? They were just at the level of my chest. I awaited the perfect moment for the maneuver. I plunged. Just at the instant when I almost had him by the legs, one of his feet slipped off the wall. He pivoted then went head over heels into space, so drunk that I'm sure I don't recall a scream.

From the eighth floor he crashed into the ground and it killed him. We heard loud screams from the street below. Everyone rushed over to see the poor Mr. Bern, who was in a terrible condition.

My God, what had come my way this evening? Everyone knew that Mr. Bern drank a lot. I felt responsible, not directly for his fall but because, hours earlier, I had refused to sign a large advance for him. He had already racked up big losses (his debt was about fifty thousand piasters, perhaps hundreds of thousands of modern-day dollars) and to me his conduct had seemed irresponsible. As director of the gaming hall I had the right to refuse this advance, thinking of course that it was, to him, rather a service. Unfortunately he played the imbecile instead, and it cost him his life. It was my sad duty to tell all that to his widow, even as I tried to console her. She was a good friend of Viane's, and I appreciated my wife's way of helping her through this. We had to file a report with the Consulate General of Great Britain. Luckily I was not lacking in witnesses, among them the *Directeur Général* of the Bank of Indochina.

*   *   *

In order to strengthen our Security Department, I succeeded in getting my friend, Chief of Police Monsieur Boubal, with concordance of the governor, to let us carry Thompson machineguns, this in addition to our Permission to Carry for revolvers which we already had. Why? My investigators had let me know that some pretty big monies were changing hands in the gaming hall.

These were monies destined to buy guns for the Vietcong. I could not interfere directly, and really I was incapable of exercising any semblance of control. The whole thing was rigged: clandestine Vietcong members would win the amount needed at a gaming table, with the complicity of some of my employees. The money then went to buy weapons. Whenever I did happen to identify someone doing this, I had him locked up... automatically.

Regrettably, when these individuals were taken out of circulation, you would "see the flipside of the medal": my Security Department's families got threatened with reprisals. This showed how gang-like the Vietcong could be.

*   *   *

When the gaming rooms closed up after hours, the gross intake of money was taken to a certain back room where it was dumped onto large tables. This made for monstrous monticules of bills. It was the same ritual every night, like supervising a cash fortune. Specialists were employed to count it, separating into piles of fifties, piles of hundreds, etcetera. The whole intake was placed into baskets, and the baskets went into lock-safes which were in the next room where there was an ultra-tight security system. In each of the four corners of the room you saw my guards armed with machineguns and ready for action. I heard that there was a Corsican Mafia which, during the prior administration, had attempted a robbery.

My nine months were up and so were my responsibilities here. Mai-Lingh always managed to be at my side, for we had become the best of friends. One day she confided that she had fallen in love with me. Oof, this was a sticky wicket. Concealing any display of emotion, I told her flat out, "Mai-Lingh, I'm married. I am faithful to my wife." I wanted nothing to do with any illicit affair.

She understood. Nevertheless, one evening, very nicely and jokingly she kissed me and said, "I know you cannot have two wives like my father. Your religion forbids it."

"Yep," I replied laughing, "it'd be a hot time in Hell."

This is the exquisite gift of jade and gold.

War Pilot Memoirs: A Mirror on 1939

CHAPTER 20

A Precious Soul enters Heaven

My Little Christiane dies of Poliomyelitis

It was Sunday, November 13, 1949. Just as it was with all the children, Christiane developed a high fever. This was not the first time, and since Viviane, with her training, was doing the nursing, the fevers usually responded to treatment. This particular day the fever did persist. We didn't get alarmed at first, but evening came with no improvement. The little girl did nothing but drink and drink, every ten minutes, which seemed normal enough with a fever, but just as soon as she drank anything it came right out the other end. Viviane and I decided to take Christiane to the Saint Paul Clinic where she was born.

Now one o'clock in the morning.

*   *   *

The doctor on duty listened to Christiane with his stethoscope. He seemed a bit worried over the little girl's condition. My little Christiane, still in my arms, started having convulsions; her temperature was very high. I was frightened and concerned, as was my wife. Attempting to reduce the child's temperature, they put us into an air conditioned room. I queried the good doctor, wanting to know what was up with my little daughter. Almost with tears in his eyes, the doctor said to me, "This is what we call 'infant paralysis', known also as poliomyelitis."

"Oh my God! What are you going to do?" I said.

After a moment of silence, he replied, "There's nothing I can do. There does not yet exist any cure. Your little one is in the hands of our Savior."

I had come through the entire War, and I had never lost courage, not even lost my cool, so oh how impossible it seemed that I was absolutely powerless to do anything for the little girl I adored. Viviane lost all control, and her wails were deafening. I was unable to hold back my tears, saying to myself, "But why, dear Lord? Why?"

The little girl's limbs were stiffening up rapidly. I did not want to let her out of my arms. I felt so very impotent as I implored all the gods of heaven to help us! Her little legs became rigid, and this paralysis rose up into her whole body. She was no longer able to move at all, not even her head. She fixed upon me a wide stare with her beautiful blue eyes, as tears rolled down her cheeks. My daughter died in my arms a few hours later. The illness had performed its ravage in eleven hours of time.

*   *   *   *

My little Christiane was buried in Saigon at the City Cemetery. I drew up her little white marble tombstone. The inscription* was:

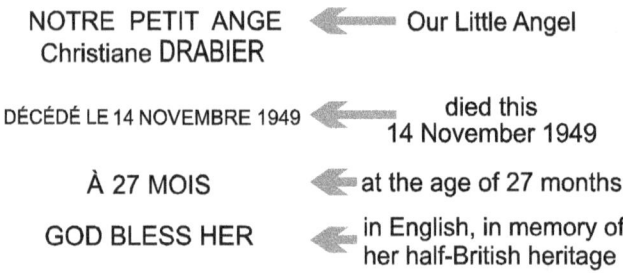

NOTRE PETIT ANGE	Our Little Angel
Christiane DRABIER	
DÉCÉDÉ LE 14 NOVEMBRE 1949	died this 14 November 1949
À 27 MOIS	at the age of 27 months
GOD BLESS HER	in English, in memory of her half-British heritage

Viviane literally got sick over it. Her health became so delicate that it worried me and my family. Doctors provided some

---

* The entire cemetery has been destroyed now, a new regime wiping out the memory of the old.

CHAPTER 20 *A Precious Soul enters Heaven*

care to get her back on her feet, but nothing was really curative. I became very concerned about my wife. I asked my mother to stick close to Viviane, to keep her company, but mostly to watch her. With my own profound sorrow, I was unable to find the strength to console my dear wife.

Since the circumstances had deteriorated so much in Saigon, even before this tragedy we had reached the decision to go back to Europe. Viviane would have been, with our little girl, off for England, and I was to have followed soon. Our little Christiane now deceased, things needed to move quicker, especially since Viviane's health was not improving. I bought a boat ticket for England by which to send my wife back to her family, noticing that the humid Indochinese climate was taking its toll worse and worse on her.

The whole of Indochina was turning to chaos with an unparalleled rapidity. The threat of war was always looming, and we were to be the losers. My instincts told me that the time was now, that it would be imprudent not to move quickly. I promised Viviane that I'd join her as soon as possible, as soon as I had my affairs in order. This was to take me about four months.

The Vietcong are Waiting for Me

Once my wife was gone I dedicated my time to the plantation. My nice little Chinese secretary, Lee-Hong of the Maritime Commerce Company of the Far East, wanted to stay with me. He was extremely devoted, so I let him. We often flew up north to inspect my plantation, walking the place together.

Before leaving Saigon to fly to the plantation, I'd usually make a phone call to my Work Supervisor there. I'd give him my estimated time of arrival so he could bring the truck with fuel for the return flight, and likewise give us a lift to the bungalow. Dang-it, this time the line was dead. I dialed the operator and was told that, along the road to Nha Trang, our army was in a battle with the Vietcong. Explosives had knocked down some phone poles. No sweat; I jumped into the plane and used its radio to raise the little shanty which was on my landing strip there.

After some bizarre chirpings over the airwaves, the response came in, "Tan Yang here." He was the Work Supervisor. He said, "Everything's ok, *Patron*. Here, everybody's left the plantation." Ok, I grabbed my suitcase. The plane loaded to the hilt, Lee-Hong and I took off. After an hour of flying we were over the airstrip, which was in the fields that we had beaten down alongside the plantation. A little wind slowed my descent just right. I put her down as usual, light on the motor, with just a few hops. Tan Yang was there with his underlings, but nobody else. I killed the motor, got out, and opened the fuselage door to remove the merchandise we had with us. Lee-Hong was helping me get the cases out.

Without our expecting it, and without any noise, straight behind us there appeared ten or twelve guys dressed in black, armed to the teeth, coming straight at us. It was too late to defend ourselves; it was too late to do anything. Right away I recognized them as Vietcong. One of them, who seemed to be the ringleader, headed straight for me. In a very good French he said, "You are our prisoners. Throw your weapons on the ground." Some of the others jumped on us, then they patted us down looking for weapons. Without really roughing us up, they tied our hands behind our backs. Very methodically they searched my plane and emptied its contents onto the ground. I could not help wondering where the tribesmen were. Had these guys killed them all?

These Vietcong guerrillas took us to the village, typically crawling with people but completely deserted now. What's more I saw inert bodies here and there. They directed us over by a tree, to which they tied us firmly. Availing myself of all the diplomacy I could muster, for purposes of stalling and putting time on our side, yet without fooling myself as to the gravity of the situation, I focused on the one who seemed to be the leader. I engaged him in conversation, saying, "What do you propose to do with us? What good would killing us be? We're not military."

He did not answer. This ringleader, rather, just wanted to play

CHAPTER 20   *A Precious Soul enters Heaven*

with my cigarette lighter. He was so amused to see flame come out of a little box. He had figured out how to throw open the flip-top lid of the lighter, a chrome metal one about the weight of a heavy pocket knife, about two inches tall, with a wick which burned petroleum fuel.

He turned his head to squint and stare at me with a look which seemed very unrighteous, then with a cocky tone he said, "Why waste any cartridges? The tigers will dispose of you tonight." What? Was this their way of getting rid of us, these renegades? I only counted about ten and I don't think there were any more. Maybe it was a little reconnaissance patrol, but one thing was strange: they were not wearing Vietcong uniforms. These were surely just village citizen sympathizers, or maybe pirates. I was overwhelmed and really wasn't coping too well with what was happening.

Anyway, we were in a pickle. Ah, the glorious fighter pilot and tiger hunter in this predicament as if in a boiling cauldron! So tigers will be the ones to gulp me down finally? I could not get over it, being so simply and stupidly tied up. No way! I did not want to end my life as an appetizer for tiger-cats!

When the guerrillas looked the other way, I'd try slipping my hands out, but there was very little chance of success. Our wrists were bloody from these bamboo strips which were tight and sharp. Night was beginning to fall, and out there we could hear the call of the wild: these beasts were not far off. That damned crew-chief came back at me, all the while puffing on his pipe, and said, "Whatever's left over of you, I'll send it to your family for breakfast." What a jerk.

Maintaining my composure, I tried once again to sweet-talk him. As my final inspiration, I played a trump card, saying, "Take my airplane. Sell it. That'll be a lot of profit for you."

He was still staring out of the corner of his eye, all arrogant. He called one of his compatriots over and gave a few orders. Pointing with his finger, then, he said, "See there what I do with your airplane." His boys, having gone over to where my plane was, lugged something resembling a case of dynamite into the interior. They lit a match and dived for cover in the brush. Pow! One enormous explosion, and my poor airplane was reduced to metal debris.

This night was pitch black, but I was able to see that the Vietcong guerrillas had slung their kitbags across their shoulders and were departing into the brush. Their mission had been accomplished. One long hour went by. Both of us, Lee-Hong and I, suffered an atrocious angst, reigned over by the black night and the stark silence of this jungle. The silence was interrupted by tigers' growling. This time, by contrast, I did not get rattled. I simply said my prayers, my Hail Marys. Our Father which art.... Ô, my Lord God, let it be that I die quickly. Of a sudden the brush around us seemed to awaken and take life. Is it tigers already? No, thank God. It was Moï tribesmen, the ones who worked my plantation! A multitude of them sprang from the brush to deliver us from a death quite certain. They soothed our bloody wrists with their medicinal herbs. They told us that when they'd bumped into the Vietcong they'd counted about ten guerrillas. They'd succeeded in killing them all using *sarbacane* blowguns. The Moï chief came up to me and handed me my gold watch, saying, "*Patron*, I think this belongs to you. The guy that had it: his throat met a knife."

The Moï chief looked out at the remnants of my airplane and realized it could no longer take me anywhere. He said, "I'll give you some men to guide you through the jungle so you can get to Saigon. They'll protect you in case of another encounter with Vietcong." Very warmly, I thanked him, but then he said to me, "Monsieur, this is a final goodbye. The Vietcong army is almost upon us. They're going to take over every plantation and village. They'll try to sweet-talk us to see us make peace with them, just so they can operate from our territory." I looked at him with tears in my eyes. I knew he was right.

Returning through brush country would be a ten-day trek, and remembering that the air time was about forty-five minutes, it

CHAPTER 20 *A Precious Soul enters Heaven* 211

was a pain. When I got to Saigon I was in one pitiful state: sick, skinned up, disoriented, feeling ruined. In Saigon, rumors were going around that the Vietcong army was nearing the city. The troops that had been fighting off this advance didn't think they could hold Saigon much longer. I found out that the Sou-Tin-Saô family had sought refuge in China. I've never managed to find any trace of them.

*   *   *

On my mother's side of the family, the Gotts were making preparations to get back to France, and my parents were already there at Angoulins-sur-mer. All Hell was breaking loose, so the Port of Saigon no longer saw any major shipping lines, and except for a few little freighters there were no ships at all. There were no more exports to load, and no passengers either.

The death of my little Christiane had messed me up, as had the departures of my wife and of my parents. I was living alone, like a crazy man, discombobulated, feeling abandoned and ruined. I was lost. Everything was rolling out of control at breakneck speed, just as in a nightmare. No more plantation, no more work, and just to top it off came this trouble transferring money out of the country! My funds were at the Bank of Indochina, and since Monsieur Sou-Tin-Saô had fled Saigon, this bank was under the directorship of a new man. It was no longer the good old bank I had known. Unfortunately it was the only bank which could make such transfers out of the country. Remember, too, that the French government of this era was Communist. There did exist a certain sentiment against colonials, not to mention the gross corruption taking hold in every administrative branch.

The governor of *Cochinchine*, Thierry d'Argenlieu, whom I knew very well, was a Gaullist. As a people, the Vietminh and the militarized Vietcong gave him plenty of grief; they had him "rewinding his bobbin" all the time, an expression we used for "troubled life."

Getting back to the international transfer of my money, there was but one organization which had the right to make colonial transfers, and it was called the Colonial Over-the-counter and Purser Bureau. Their cut was fifty percent of whatever got transferred! To boot, there was no guarantee that the money would reach its destination. Not only had I lost everything, but now I learned they'd be taking scissors to every bill and not even promising that I'd see my half again. What a sham. I felt like <u>not</u> going back to France. I was downhearted. I had no future. After years of hard work and hoping to secure an endowment for my wife and family, I was without hope. I had nothing. But I still had my pride... so, what to do? I made one very risky decision which would carry me through to my final days in Indochina. To make things right, I wanted to avenge this country which I loved so dearly.

The Vietcong were bound and determined to stamp me out. Cost me what it may, I decided to regain the upper hand and defend my birthright. Vietcong insurgents had learned of my working relationship with the governor and with his intelligence agency. Truth be told, monetarily I was tapped out. I wanted to come by some money, at least enough to get me back to Europe.

The Governor and my Interview

I reached an accord with the governor to help him infiltrate a clandestine print shop, and I would provide him with the relevant addresses and proof. It was being run by the Vietcong and was situated right in the middle of Saigon. Using the print shop to further their political agenda, they were scam artists to boot. At this shop, I knew the names of two individuals who were Vietcong agents, and these individuals were employees of the governor himself! I was to deliver these shady characters into the hands of the proper authorities. The governor assigned two bodyguards to be at my disposal, and they accompanied me everywhere, 24 hours a day. They carried machineguns and other heavy weapons.

To define this mission, I signed a contract with the governor.

CHAPTER 20   *A Precious Soul enters Heaven*   213

By virtue of this I found myself on the Vietcong "red list", their hit list, with honorable mention: Most Wanted. I must say I found anew all my combat skill and thinking, and in short order. With my two guys who were former commandos, the three of us were pretty formidable. We had an eye toward every hideout, and, just like walking point, one of us was on the lookout every moment of the day. Since I didn't have a car now, we traveled by rickshaw, or by bicycle. When the print shop was seized, three workers were arrested and sent to prison. This was my first triumph. Following this, as agreed, I did receive substantial remuneration from Governor d'Argenlieu, all of which led to an attempt, in Saigon, on my life.

This particular day I wanted to go to the open-air flower market, just twenty minutes away from where I lived. It was a friend's birthday. I said to my guards, "I won't need you. I'll be out in the crowd. I'll take a rickshaw." Generally, as a safety habit, we used the same rickshaw drivers. These hearty souls knew us and knew our routine, so we had no trouble. Bizarre thing this particular day: that guy didn't look familiar to me. I started out, bound for the Boulevard Charner where the open-air market was, despite my feeling that something was wrong. The rickshaw driver took a so-called shortcut, which seemed even more bizarre, but since I knew this roadway I didn't let it bother me. We were to traverse a distance the length of three football fields, with no traffic and no people. It was off the beaten path, a sort of park with a lot of bushes and trees on either side of the street. It wouldn't be but five minutes to get across that stretch, yet, halfway, a terrible urge to urinate overcame me. I told the boy to stop, and in good French tradition, which is to say in keeping with our simplistic views on toileting, I set my sights on a tree thirty feet away. I figured that'll do fine seeing as how there's no one around. I stepped up to the tree and relieved myself.

My driver was crouched down beside the towing members of his rickshaw. He was waiting for me, when… abruptly… a chill ran down my spine. While I was pulling up my zipper: flack! A knife came to rest in the bark of the tree with its handle still vibrating right by my cheek! Wow. I turned quickly, my .38 caliber in hand. It was my own rickshaw driver who had thrown the knife! There was no one else anywhere near, so as soon as he realized he'd missed me, he drew a second knife and was preparing to launch it. By good fortune, before he could finish his throw... I was quicker than he was. I brought him down, and the noise from my revolver drew a small crowd. Among them was a French soldier, so to him I quickly displayed my national ID card which gave my profession, Maritime Agent. I told him, "That was a close call," and he was sympathetic. On the indigenous boy he found a Vietcong ID card with the kid's military number and a photo of Ho Chi Minh.

From that day onward I swore never to venture out without my bodyguards. It was of utmost importance that I keep two things in my head: that I was on a mission, and that I had become a daily target for the Vietcong.

*   *   *

On one more occasion I must say my guardian angel protected me. To understand how this one came down, let me describe the place where I was living. My bedroom window overlooked a short little street, about fifty yards long, which formed a "T" intersection with a major street called *rue Pellerin*. My apartment, then, was on a dead-end street. This particular afternoon the weather was really hot, so it was a particularly good time for a siesta. I was seated on the edge of my bed, daydreaming for a moment before stretching out. The wooden shutters on my window were closed to make it dark, which took the edge off the heat. With the shutters closed I was not able to see the street. I had just stretched out when a spray of machinegun bullets pierced the shutters! I rolled out, knowing that if I had only taken one more moment before stretching out, I would have been scissors-cut in two. Both my bodyguards, who were in the next room, sprang into action with machineguns in hand. Quickly realizing

CHAPTER 20 *A Precious Soul enters Heaven*

what had happened, kicking open the shutters with the blow of one foot, they fired into the street. The perpetrators' shadows were the only things left to receive the gunfire; they had fled.

This time the Vietcong had planned well, but they had been foiled by my guardian angel. They wanted me dead at any price. I hope I've adequately described how tightly the Vietcong were monitoring me.

Three attempts: first the episode in the jungle, second the knife-throw and third the spray of machinegun bullets. What, then, would be the nature of the next one? I was impressed that their methods came in such a multitude.

When surrounded by a crowd, we felt safer. Many civilians were carrying weapons, perpetrators knew this, so a crowd was a blanket of security. Perpetrators would not put themselves at risk opening fire in a crowd. On the other hand you avoided getting off in a spot that wasn't frequented. This could be problematic, even dangerous.

I was happy that my assignment was drawing to an end, and that I was still alive. There was just one more thing to be done: buy me a boat ticket to England, and posthaste. The only ship that still came our way was the *SS Falstria*, a Danish freighter. Darn: it wouldn't be in for two weeks. I hoped to see my "final bullet" reach its mark, to see me successfully fulfill the governor's mission, because otherwise I would have to go without a paycheck.

*   *   *

The Vietcong had not exhausted their efforts. This time they showed extreme ingenuity to get me. I never will know how they organized this, but I do know how close they came to succeeding.

One morning, I was out of condensed milk for my coffee. I sent one of my bodyguards to the little Chinese grocer around the corner from where I lived. For quite some time I had been trading there. While waiting for him to get back, I petted my little black kitty-cat which had been with me through some difficult times. Cats can be soothing. My bodyguard got back with two cans of condensed milk, the same brand name which I always got.

My bodyguard recounted an unordinary chain of events. The owner of the little store had not been in, so another guy, whom my guard didn't know, had waited on him. My guard had been required to stand and wait while the employee went to the back end of the store for the milk. Finally, the employee had come back smiling, cans of milk in hand. My guard said to me, "I don't know why he went to the back. There were cans right there on the shelf." Well, I just listened, not finding anything to say for the moment. There must have been a reason.

We opened up one can and I poured some into my coffee. Boy, it did smell good. I leaned over to take a sip. Oops, too hot. I'd wait and let it cool down. Leaving the cup of coffee on the kitchen table, I went into the next room to talk over our upcoming mission with my bodyguards. Five minutes went by, when all of a sudden we heard frantic meowing, as if someone had stomped on the kitty-cat's tail. We heard fracas and scuffling, something bouncing around on the floor, then silverware and plates falling. I raised an eyebrow and asked myself what in the world this cacophony could be. Why is my cat acting like such an imbecile? We went into the kitchen, getting there just in time to see the cat, four paws in the air, convulsing violently. This gave way to one final lunge, then stillness. He was dead! All three of us looked at each other, dumbfounded.

On the table we noticed that my coffee cup, filled to the brim before, was now half empty. There were some drops of coffee on the floor near the cat. The kitty must have lapped up some of my café-au-lait. What the devil had happened? We looked at each other, perplexed, then we said as if with one voice, "Poison." But how was that possible? I'd been using this same container of coffee for over a week without any trouble. The <u>milk</u>! We had

CHAPTER 20   *A Precious Soul enters Heaven*

just opened this can of milk, so it would have been impossible for someone to put something into it. We didn't theorize any further. We took the coffee, milk… cat, and all, to the Pasteur Institute laboratory to have an analysis done. It didn't take long for them to deduce there was arsenic in the milk; there was enough to poison a whole regiment!

At the lab, they explained to us the trick which had been employed to inject poison into cans of condensed milk. For purposes of the manufacturing process, on the top of each metal can there was a tiny hole, barely visible to the naked eye. The hole was there to allow the quality of the milk to be checked at random during the manufacturing process, whereby a syringe might be pushed through this hole to take out some milk to be analyzed. At a certain point in time, the hole would be soldered shut, leaving only a tiny half millimeter of solder.

Now I was starting to get it: the Vietcong had used the same method to inject arsenic into the can of condensed milk! This was mysterious: how could they know that I would drink this particular can? Was all the milk on the shelves of that little store contaminated? There must have been thirty cans or more. Could they all contain poison?

Every can of milk in the place got gathered up for analysis: they all were normal. Now I remembered how my bodyguard had told me about the guy's going to the back of the store to get two cans, and how he had taken a good bit of time. That must have been when he'd injected poison into the milk. Immediately we alerted the police, who went with us to the Chinese grocer's. They arrested him and his accomplice and placed them in the military jail.

*   *   *

Once again, I had experienced a narrow escape. It was thanks to my little cat that lost his life in saving mine. I'll gladly admit the whole thing gave me the shivers. I became afraid of everything. No matter where I was, if I ate or drank anything, it was a cause for trepidation.

Finally I wrapped up my assignment successfully, and the governor paid me for my service. Now I had just one thing on the brain, one sole mission to fulfill: getting out of this country! Yet this was the country <u>where I was born</u>, the country which I cherished.

Saigon: Christiane (last photo before her departure) and mother Viviane

War Pilot Memoirs: A Mirror on 1939

CHAPTER 21

Dénouement: Nightmares on a Danish Cargo Ship

My whole family had already left Indochina: parents, uncles, aunts, cousins, friends. I was leaving as a ruined man, with nothing to carry away but my memories. To myself I was saying, "I may be ruined, but I'm alive. Not all is lost." At least I had my memories, fragments of recollections of days gone by. I had a lump in my throat, with a firm, albeit intuitive, feeling that never again would I see my native land.

Not simply a get-up-and-go, my departure aboard the *SS Falstria*, a Danish cargo ship, was a clandestine operation. Nighttime: 6 January, 1951. Other passengers boarded in the usual fashion, but I was taken to the ship in a dingy. The *SS Falstria* was at anchor in the middle of the port. For security reasons, to keep things quiet, they paddled me out there with no motor. I carried, all told and sum total, a little suitcase and my revolvers. This was it, the remainder of the sizeable fortune I had amassed here. That particular night I could hear explosions all over Saigon. There were fires, and gunshots, with whistling bullets making themselves heard everywhere.

We weighed anchor at dawn. My God, I cannot fully express the pain and sadness I felt. I was heartbroken, leaving behind my dearest, most cherished Christiane, there in that most beautiful cemetery* in Saigon! I was so depressed that I found myself even unable to cry.

The freighter took at least three hours to make it down the Mekong River and out into the open ocean. It was a modern enough vessel for its era. For example, it had electric cranes which helped it load up in relative silence, compared to those noisy steam cranes, so this vessel was ok for passengers. There were about fifty cabins, all of the same class and very comfortable. I was worn out, beaten down, crippled with fatigue, stressed out, but most of all nervous. I compare it to a time of convalescing which is getting off to a bad start.

My first night was one terrible ordeal. Just as was my custom, I went to bed with two revolvers under my pillow. My sleep was agitated. I woke up often, and all sweaty. I sat up, my back leaning against the wall of the cabin at the head of my bed. I was just coming out of a bad dream. At that moment, thinking I heard something threatening, I grabbed my two revolvers and pointed them at the door of the cabin! What I did not realize was that my back, pressed against the wall that way, was pushing a button to ring for service. I heard knocking, knocking, knocking at my door… my reaction was to freeze. I still had the two pistols in my hands, my eyes in a wide-eyed stare. They kept knocking… then knocked some more. Finally a key was inserted into the keyhole and the door opened. When the female attendant saw me, holding my two revolvers and with a wild look on my face, she was taken off guard. She ran screaming down the corridor.

In the interest of keeping order onboard, a purser came right away. It was the Ship Security Officer. He had a bottle of champagne in one hand, and the other hand he stretched out for me to shake. He understood what was going on, therefore, very nicely and calmly, he said, "It's alright, Monsieur Drabier, you're safe here. Put down your weapons. All is secure. Calm down, I'm your friend." Then he came over beside me, took my pistols and

---

* Our friends visited Saigon in 2008, finding that the Communist regime had destroyed this cemetery to erase memories of the colonial era. The Le Van Tam Park is there now.

CHAPTER 21 *Dénouement: Nightmares on a Danish Cargo Ship*

told me, "You'll not be needing these here. You can pick them up again when we reach England." He kept speaking ever so gently as he slipped the revolvers from my hands. He poured some champagne into a glass for me.

Finally I regained my composure, I sincerely begged forgiveness, then I said, "Alright. Alright." This ship's officer was very likeable. He was up to date on events in Indochina and knew what I must have been through. He understood my reaction. Again he poured me some champagne, and this time we drank together. I thanked him for his courtesy and his presence of mind. And such was the way I departed Indochina.

*   *   *

The trip was long, yet agreeable; anyway, 1951 saw me back in England. I call the trip long for the great number of ports we had to visit. After leaving Saigon, these were the points on the chart: the section of Malaysia adjoining Borneo, the port city of Singapore, then the western part of Malaysia on the peninsula, the island of Pinang, the city of Rangoon in the country of Burma also called Myanmar, the city of Colombo on the island of Ceylon, the city of Aden in the country of Yemen where we had to take on diesel fuel, and boy it did stink. While they were refueling the ship, to help us passengers pass the time, snake charmers came aboard to entertain us. This was actually a premise for selling us their wristwatches, trinkets and chatch-kees.

The ship set out again, straight for the Suez Canal. One stop at the city of Port Said in Egypt, then we traversed the whole Mediterranean to get to the city of Tangiers in the country of Morocco. We chugged along the coast of Portugal on the Atlantic, then the Atlantic coast of France to reach the city of Brest in the region of Brittany. Our final run was over to the city of Southampton in England. From there I took a train to the city of Horsham, Sussex County, where Viviane was waiting for me with the whole Wells family, minus her father, sad to say.

The food served onboard this Danish freighter was really tasty, copious and of good quality. Truth be told, such good eats had been a missing factor in my life for quite some time. What's more there was nothing to <u>do</u> onboard this freighter. No longer fearing Vietcong attacks, I gorged myself on all these tasty things. This did put a good ten pounds onto my small frame. Result? I could just barely button my pants. *Quelle horreur*!*

The *SS Falstria* of Denmark

* "Oh, man. Such a pity. What a shame."

Acknowledgements

Such a book could never have seen the light of day without the help of many people, first and foremost, my devoted wife Janine. Her keyboard skills allowed us to make headway, and she had patience with me as I wrestled with words to express memories long forgotten.

I thank General William Anders for his personal words of support which got me started.

I acknowledge the honorary Mayor of Douarnenez, Monsieur Michel Mazéas, who was at the dock when the *Trébouliste* set sail in the wee hours of June 19th, 1940, and with whom I have established contact in modern times.

Je remercie la famille Tackoen pour leur aide à la recherche de la tombe de ma petite Christiane à Saigon.*

I acknowledge my Free French Air Force comrades, too numerous to name. My lifelong colleague André Voirin is a hero among helicopter pilots and a beloved friend.

I thank my professional readers, Mary Aycock, a cost accountant and avid reader, plus Damon English, representative for Aflac and a military historian.

I acknowledge the Arnett family of 492ndBombGroup.com, and of documentary film fame, for research.

Finally I wish to thank *Monsieur le professeur* John D. Hodges, whom I found through Glendale Community College, for his diligence. I grant him the right to use this material for publication in the event of my demise.

---

* I thank the Tackoen family for their help in looking for the tomb of my little Christiane in Saigon.

www.ingramcontent.com/pod-product-compliance
Lightning Source LLC
Chambersburg PA
CBHW031138160426
43193CB00008B/184